© Copyright 2022 - Al

The content contained within this I
duplicated or transmitted without dire
author or the publisher.

Under no circumstances will any blame or legal responsibility be held against the publisher, or author, for any damages, reparation, or monetary loss due to the information contained within this book, either directly or indirectly.

Legal Notice:

This book is copyright protected. It is only for personal use. You cannot amend, distribute, sell, use, quote or paraphrase any part, or the content within this book, without the consent of the author or publisher.

Disclaimer Notice:

Please note the information contained within this document is for educational and entertainment purposes only. All effort has been executed to present accurate, up to date, reliable, complete information. No warranties of any kind are declared or implied. Readers acknowledge that the author is not engaged in the rendering of legal, financial, medical or professional advice. The content within this book has been derived from various sources. Please consult a licensed professional before attempting any techniques outlined in this book.

By reading this document, the reader agrees that under no circumstances is the author responsible for any losses, direct or indirect, that are incurred as a result of the use of the information contained within this document, including, but not limited to, errors, omissions, or inaccuracies.

This book is dedicated to my wonderful loving wife Jo for her ceaseless encouragement, patience & endless devotion - and to our amazing creative, creations Yanina & Gyorg - You are my inspiration !

Table of Contents

OF COWS AND COWHIDE 1

CHAPTER 1: BOVINE BEHEMOTHS ON THE BRAIN—COW CONSCIOUSNESS 3

    COW PATS AND PATTING COWS: UNGULATES AND URBANITES 3
    UDDER NONSENSE: MILK—FROM TEAT TO TEA 4
    PABLO PICASSO TO GARY LARSON: HOW COWS HAUNT OUR NIGHTMARES 6
    BULLSHIT, BULLS, AND BEARS: HOW COWS HAVE IMPACTED THE ENGLISH LANGUAGE......... 8
    GRAZE AND GAZE: LIVING UNDER BOVINE SCRUTINY 9

CHAPTER 2: CAVES, COWS, AND CARVED COLUMNS 11

    AUROCHS & LASCAUX: THE HALL OF THE BULLS 11
    DAIRY DEITIES? THE CULT OF THE COSMIC COW 12
    THE FIRST COWBOYS: WHEN HUMANS FIRST HERDED CATTLE... 13
    TOLLUND MAN'S HOOD AND ÖTZI THE ICEMAN'S NICE LEATHER SHOELACES.................... 15
    LEATHER LEAVES AND COWHIDE COVERS 16

CHAPTER 3: CONSUMING COWS AND WORLD CULTURES—1,000 WAYS TO EAT A COW 19

    ROAST BEEF AND THE ENGLISH ARTERIES 20
    SLABS OF STEAK AND MOUNTAINS OF MINCE: THE AMERICAN EXPERIENCE...................... 21
    DAINTY EATERS: HOW THE THAI EAT THE LEAST POSSIBLE BEEF 22
    WAGYU: MARVELOUS MARBLING ON THE MENU 23
    MILK AND BLOOD—MAASAI CATTLE 24
    LA VACHE FRANÇAISE: COW-EATING IN FRANCE 25
    EATING COWS IN INDIA? 25
    A THOUSAND WAYS TO EAT A COW 26

CHAPTER 4: BESIDES BEEF—LEATHER FOR THE LEATHERMAN.......................... 27

    THE INNER REALITY OF COW SKIN 27
    THE HISTORY OF HERBIVORE HIDE-HACKS.. 28
        Protective Equipment 28
        Industrial Applications 29
        Domestic Use 30
        Military Applications.. 30
        On the Farm 32
        Sport, Leisure, and Cows 32
        Hospitals and Hide.. 33

FROM FOUR FEET TO TWO: WHY JIMMY CHOO LOVES COWS 33
    Fancy Footwear *33*
    Fabulous Fashion *34*

CHAPTER 5. DEM BONES, DEM BONES, DEM COW BONES 37

WHY WASTE ANYTHING? 37
    Of Cows, Dogs, and Dynamite *37*
    Movie Props to Jelly Tots *38*
    Jet Fuel to Josiah Spode *39*
    Heifers, Highways, and High-End Cars *39*
    Fertilizer and Charcoal *40*
    The Future of the Cow Bone Industry? *40*
WHERE THERE'S MUCK THERE'S MONEY: THE VALUE OF COW POO 41
AND IN CONCOWSION... 42

CHAPTER 6: POO TO PRADA—THE STINKY SKILLS OF CURING COWHIDE 43

A SHOUT OUT FOR THE TRADITIONAL TANNERS 43
    Willows, Tea, and Tannin' Hides *43*
    Wrangling Raw Cowhide *44*
TECHNICAL TANNING: SLUDGY SKIN TO LOVELY LEATHER 46
BEAMHOUSE OPERATIONS 47
FINDING A TANNERY NEAR YOU! 48
AN ALDEHYDE-TO-ZEOLITE OF TANNING OPTIONS 49

CHAPTER 7: TRAINING IN THE TRICKS OF THE TRADE 51

UNIVERSITY DAYS 51
PENDRAGON, WALES, AND LUSCIOUS LEATHER LOUNGEWEAR 52
THE *OTHER* LEATHER SMELL 54
BLEMISHED AND UNBLEMISHED: LIFETIME MARKS A COW 56
EXPERIENCES OF AN APPY UPHOLSTERY DESIGNER 58
    Of Chainmail and Leather Cutters *58*
    Stitching Up *59*
    Sofa Stuffing *60*
THE HALLMARKS OF GREAT LEATHER UPHOLSTERY 60

CHAPTER 8: SEEKING HIDE—SELECTING LEATHER 63

THE SPLIT PERSONALITY OF COMMERCIAL LEATHER: LEATHER AND LEATHER SPLIT 63
    Hide: Layer upon Layer upon Layer *63*
    Splitting Hairs over Hides *64*
FINISHING FLOURISHES: DELIGHTFUL AND DAFT 66
FASHION TRENDS IN COW-SITTING 67
IT'S ALL ABOUT THE ANIMAL 70

CHAPTER 9: IT'S A HARD KNOCK LIFE FOR THE HERBIVORE 71

    Highland Coos and Assorted Moos: An International Alphabet of Cows 72
    Leather Terroir? Unique Properties of Unique Meadows 73
    Happy Herds of Contented Cows? 74
        Cow-Drink 74
        Cow-Food 75
        Cow-Vitamins 75
        Medical Aid for Cows 76
    A Whole Range of Cattle Ranges 77

CHAPTER 10: ALTERNATIVE COWS—A LEATHER SUBSTITUTE? 81

    Farting Cows and Greenhouse Gasses 81
        The Cow's Carbon Hoofprint 82
        The Hunter's Off-Set? 82
    Poison Oozes Where Regulation Snoozes 83
    Ruminants vs. Rainforests? 84
    Leather Ethics 84
        Leather is Part of Our Human Heritage 85
        Leather is a Circular Resource 85
        Carbon Off-Setting 85
        Less Beef and Less Leather 85
        Transparent Supply Chains 85
        Costed-in Sustainability 86
        Change in Positioning 86
        Encouraging—Not Resisting—Research 86
        Open to Innovation 86
    Alternative Armchairs for the Anthropoid Arse 86
        Polymers 87
        Natural Fibers and—Sand? 87
    Bottom Line—the Bovine Balance 88

SITTING COMFORTABLY 89

REFERENCES 91

Of Cows and Cowhide

My name is Matt Arquette and I'm a furniture designer! My specialty is upholstery furniture design and has been for at least 20 years. At 43, and with 44 encroaching, I have spent half my life in designing and creating upholstery furniture. Now it's time to share my obsessive pleasure with you!

For those that don't know what upholstery is—it's taking a bunch of sticks, a few slabs of foam (and sometimes some springs), and wrapping them up in a cover often made of that pliable paragon of materials, leather!

Of course, it's ever so slightly more complex than that. There's creating the shape according to design, choosing the right foam to stuff it with, and most importantly, choosing the right cover. The cover is that part of the furniture your body will make contact with during the sensuous experience of sitting.

In this book I am particularly focusing on leather. In the future, I have every intention of investigating our peculiar relationships with cotton and threads that derive from the arse of bugs. Work is already in progress on exciting topics like *The Quintessential Chesterfield Sofa*, *Smart Furniture, the Future*, *From Spitfire to Sofa*, and lots more! For now, though, I want to look more deeply at our insatiable desire for the cow, and how we use her hides to plushly plump our environments!

My interest is the interface between cow bum and human bum—this is an investigation into sitting on cows.

Facts about Matt Arquette

- International Furniture Designer, born in 1979 in UK
- Bachelor of Arts Honors Degree—UCE Birmingham Institute of Art & Design
- Design Director & Founder of Mash + Designs UK
- Design Director & Founder of M + Design Solutions Hong Kong
- Chief Designer for DeRucci—Lamborghini—V6 & Calia Italia Furniture Ranges
- Design Director and co-founder of MQUETTE Smart Furniture
- Head of Design for Morgan House Luxury Furnishings
- Expert International Cow-sitter!

Matt Arquette has been designing furniture internationally for over 20 years. He has won many prestigious awards, and his unique style is widely sought after by world class retailers and manufacturers alike, from Ikea to Lamborghini. Matt pursues his enjoyment for design enthusiastically, sharing his passion for freshness in furniture conceptualization. Always thinking beyond the conventional but never exceeding functionality, each style he creates always maintains personality and uniqueness.

Although he is a funny man, he's completely serious about high-quality furniture.

Chapter 1:

Bovine Behemoths on the Brain—

Cow Consciousness

We are conditioned by the animals we embrace. Humans domesticated dogs and became more dog-like. Cats domesticated us and became more human-like. We domesticated cattle, and now look at us—nothing gives us more pleasure than snuggling up to real cows, skin to skin.

Cow Pats and Patting Cows: Ungulates and Urbanites

The average urbanite never encounters a warm, living, breathing cow. And yet, cows impinge on our lives from infancy. Children's books are full of cute cows. Wallpapers are plastered with cows improbably jumping over moons. We play with farm sets and chew plastic cows from our earliest years. Cows are always in the background as a benign bovine presence, comforting and far too domesticated to ever trample our flower beds.

I really want to introduce you to this wonderful *animal*. It's true that they are part of our cultural consciousness, but they are *not* mythical beasts. They are living, breathing sharers of our planet, and we should grow into an adult appreciation of them for who they really are, not for who they represent. We do that with our parents, so why not with our farm sets?

Let's start with that convincing sign of real existence that will forever distinguish the cow from the tooth fairy. Cows leave cowpats behind, not money under your pillow.

My first encounter with cow dung as a small town boy was whilst on holiday in Wales. I came across these dryish, circular, fibrous artifacts on the ground. What were they? At that stage my mind had nowhere to file them. They were dotted all over the field we were camped in. After curiously probing one with a stick and inhaling its heady aroma I could confirm it was certainly poo of some description. I invited my younger brother to investigate further. I launched a heavy stone onto the crusty disk which delightfully broke, spraying its gooey contents all over him. At first he was too busy laughing to realize he could do the same to me. Then, he did. Splat! We both had our first taste of cow pat, a hilarious moment of enlightenment for two small boys!

A friend of mine who grew up on a farm told me about "cow pat socks." He describes walking around barefoot on a frosty morning, where a big pleasure for him and his sisters would be to find a fresh cowpat, and snuggle their cold-numb toes into its steamy warmth to get the feeling back into their feet. This broadened my perceptions with regard to the versatility of everything related to cows!

It took me a while to learn the facts of life and the reality of cows. It is a typical urban story that the first time I got to pat a calf and let it suck my fingers was when I was already at the uni!

Udder Nonsense: Milk—From Teat to Tea

Another sign of the reality of cows is the existence of milk, although some deny its rural origins. Dairy Flat-Earthers propose that milk is synthesized in secret caverns beneath supermarkets by chemical engineers.

Only a privileged few global urbanites have survived an actual milking-of-cows experience and lived to tell the tale. I am one of them, and I can testify that milk *does* come from the pink teats and bulgy udders of real cows! In the time of Thomas Hardy, the Victorian novelist, the milk industry required an army of highly skilled milking professionals (a.k.a. milkmaids. They were at the bottom of the rural income pyramid—see Hardy's famous milkmaid story, *Tess of the d'Urbervilles*). Nowadays a single dairyperson can often cope with milk-time on their own, with the aid of a many-tentacled milking machine.

An active dairy on a dairy farm is an astonishingly clean place. It has to be, or Tesco won't come and collect your milk to sell. Everything gets sprayed with water and disinfectant. The cows amble in, and while they settle down to a nice snack, the dairyperson attaches a set of four suction cups to each udder. The machine then empties each ungulate udder in a time neatly calculated for each cow to finish her feed. While this is all happening, the cows unselfconsciously confirm their real existence by defecating into the dedicated slurry channel. When the milk is all garnered, they get detached from the machine and thoughtfully amble out to pasture. The dairyperson swooshes the slurry out to the slurry-pit, and then hoses down everything again with water and disinfectant. Then they hitch up everything to an automatic sterilization process, run on the same principles as your dentist's machinery, interestingly enough.

Thanks to Louis Pasteur, the milk is then heated up to 63°C in a system of stainless steel pipes, plates, and tanks, ready for the milk truck to collect it for bottling, bagging, and boxing. We should be grateful to Louis. Although some people swear by the health benefits of raw milk, the pasteurization process thwarts the ambition of some mean little pathogens which thrive on raw milk and have a deep desire to make human life miserable. I prefer not to encounter Mycobacterium tuberculosis, Salmonella spp., enteropathogenic E. coli, Campylobacter jejuni, and Listeria monocytogenes in my cereal bowl (Oraon, 2013).

Strangely enough, though, the ubiquity of milk in our diet does not win the case for the reality of cows (although it ought to)! City children chomp through their breakfasts of processed grains softened by milk without consciously making the pink-teat connection. Their parents moderate the bitterness of their caffeine-rich morning drinks of choice with judicious sloshes of the stuff. And yet, everybody acts as though drinking the secretions of bovine mammary glands is unexceptional.

It is. What an extraordinary world we live in.

Pablo Picasso to Gary Larson: How Cows Haunt Our Nightmares

Enlightenment to the corporeal reality of cows is often sadly accompanied by a loss of faith in their benevolence. They cease to be as safe as they seemed. Once you get up close to a living cow, you realize how *very* much larger they are than us. They might be calmly licking up large mouthfuls of meadow, but when you get near them, you realize that your parents perpetrated a dangerous deception with the plastic cow of your farmyard set. In the animal world, cows are *big* animals. We are *small* animals.

Cows are dangerous because of this mass differential. I grew up in a small market town in Worcestershire, where they know how to spin a farmer's yarn. I remember hearing with horror how a cowman got his current position on a dairy farm because a cow had unthinkingly lent against the previous cowman, in a companionable sort of way. There was a wall on the other side. The man was quietly and good-naturedly crushed to death! Anybody who has inadvertently found themselves surrounded by a herd of Charolais cattle whilst on a stroll through the countryside might relate to this menace. Vast walls of bulky beef loom up on either side of the puny human ramblers. Accidents can happen if something spooks the herd!

Of course, cows are usually truly placid, and carry their bulk with no actual malice. That does not hold for Mr. Cow, though! Bulls are primed by eons of evolution to protect their herd from predators and other bulls. They are also blessed with very little brain. In addition, that little brain is preoccupied by thoughts of sex and eating. There is nothing in this limited cognitive capacity to allow a bull to not think of you as either a predator or a competitor. Some urbanites learn this too late.

Fortunately, due to artificial insemination, there were only 295 breeding bulls in all of England in 2020 (Department for Environment, Food & Rural Affairs, 2021). However, a steady trickle of MOPs (as the Health And Safety Executive of the Agriculture Industry Advisory Committee endearingly calls "Members of the Public") get hurt or killed by cattle every year (AIAC, 2020). You need to take cows seriously if they threaten to turn you into a government statistic!

Becoming aware of this danger has given rise to what I consider to be the *Minotaur World*, the dark background to some of our worst nightmares (not "nightcows" for some inscrutable reason).

Ever since the 14 cow-power nightmare of Pharaoh in the Hebrew Scriptures, cows have haunted our dreams. The contrast of their bigness and wildness to our smallness and tameness has generated ambivalent feelings that have tormented us with night-time terror. Children have comforting cows in fluffy fabric to sleep with. Adults get horrible horned cows to wake them up sweating!

The Minotaur is the archetype of this nightmarish landscape, the bull-man fusion that lurks in the heart of the maze and feasts on whoever gets lost in it. It takes the superhuman strength of Theseus and the clever use of a ball of string to kill this beast. But nightmares never truly die, and the two recent dreamers who have caught this are Pablo Picasso and Gary Larson.

Pablo was a tiny little Spaniard who obsessed over painting big burly bulls (overcompensating much?). His nightmare vision of "the bull" runs through many of his surreal paintings. His 1945 series of 11 lithographs show the progressive paring down of a bull to its horrific abstracted essentials, and left him with an ideogram of bullishness that ran through much of the rest of his work. Of course, that bull nightmare had already been in his head in 1937 (in his Guernica). Perhaps he suffered from Tauromania, if that's a thing? If you are a horror addict, by all means order some Picasso prints and paper your study with them.

Another expositor of the bovine nightmare is Gary Larson. In his surreal world cows cross the boundary between bovinanity and humanity to become actors in our everyday spheres of life. They welcome guests to their suburban homes and barbecue steaks (!) on their back lawns (to the indignation of their bovine neighbors). They drive in cars and observe humans in fields, and send their calves to schools like everyone else. It is not only humor based on placidly jolly inversions—Larson shows how cows send agents to burn down Chicago, and how mad scientists stitch together pieces from the butchery to create reanimated monsters. Do not let your toddler in her moo-cow pajamas get hold of your Gary Larson collection too young!

Bullshit, Bulls, and Bears: How Cows Have Impacted the English Language

It was the Norman invaders who fueled our contemporary urban isolation from actual cows. Part of the reason that we only have a vestigial memory of cattle is rooted in the defeat of King Harold Arrow-Eye in 1066. When the new lordlings took over the management of England, they all snobbily spoke French to each other. English was the language of the servants, a secret language in which cooks and milkmaids could swear at their upper class oppressors.

This is reflected in the English language, and reflects the social realities of a millennium ago. The serf herding bovine meat on the hoof called the animal "a cow" in good old Anglo Saxon English. The serf was unlikely, though, to get any of that cow to eat. When, in due course, that bovine protein appeared in steaming, fatty lumps lathered with gravy on the tables of the great, it underwent a language shift to "du boeuf." God forbid that it retain any of the flavor of cow dung and English!

This is only one way in which cows, which are generally inarticulate, have influenced the way we think and talk.

Think about it.

We describe somebody as being "led by the nose"—even though none of us has watched a farmhand maneuver a bull ten times his weight by casually pulling it along by a ring through its sensitive nose. An actress 'milks' the opportunity for attention on a red carpet, even though she would shudder at an udder in real life. When we want to insult the lack of innovation and reluctance to initiate change in our government, we accuse them of having a "herd mentality." Cowboys have all the Halloween leather glamor and shooting skills, and hardly anyone expects to find them out persuading actual cows to move in the right direction.

Bulls glare at bears in our stock markets, although nobody can remember when livestock was last traded at the world's stock exchanges. And we admire something being as tough as old boots, although even Mythbusters hasn't tested out why old boots should be the industry standard for rugged durability! And why O why would a bull ever get through the door of a chinashop?

Cows have left their large cloven hoofprints all over our language. That isn't bullshit either!

Graze and Gaze: Living Under Bovine Scrutiny

While we are looking closely at them, remember that cows are looking curiously right back at us! They find us particularly interesting if we produce some sort of music—bagpipe reels perhaps, piano accordion medleys, or even trumpet concertos. Cattle are apparently not doing anything with the information they are so patiently gathering (yet! as Gary Larson might warn us). They simply seem to like a little light entertainment, and humans are just the sort of performing monkeys they can appreciate. If ever you feel depressed about your lack of achievement in life, ponder this: You are a fully qualified and deeply appreciated cow-entertainer. Get in your car and drive a couple of hours to find an attentive audience in a meadow near you. You don't need to actually be able to *play* an instrument. Just take one along with you and you're golden.

Whenever I have met cows I have been impressed by their undemanding brown-eyed gaze. To me they are soothing, even soporific, so long as there is a solid fence between us. But not everyone shares my point of view.

Our highly intelligent human minds are so highly strung that some of us have been known to develop a deep irrational fear of cows. It has two names in the psychiatric literature: Bovinophobia from Latin, and Taurophobia from Greek. It is defined as "the excessive (and often irrational) fear of cows or cattle" (Olesen, 2020), and the unfortunate people who are tormented by this syndrome experience "intense, excessive and persistent worry and fear about cows, often involving repeated episodes of sudden feelings of intense anxiety and fear or terror that reach a peak within minutes" (Mayo Clinic, 2018).

I was gobsmacked when I discovered this! I must emphasize that I am not speaking as a medical expert here in any way, but it seems to my uneducated understanding that there are realistically only two ways to deal with Bovinophobia. Firstly, stick to towns wherever you go, and only visit places with guaranteed zero populations of cattle (like Antarctica). Or else, secondly, whenever you emerge from towns into the rural wastelands between them, wear one of those fluffy cow onesies that were popular a while back. That way you will blend into the herd, and no cow will look at you twice.

And for your comfort, you are not alone. The most reckless of sub-superheroes, Deadpool himself, is the poster-boy for Bovinophobia. He says cows "scare the ℂRsA £ outta" him, always "watching and waiting."

Which is only the truth. There is always a cow watching!

Chapter 2:

Caves, Cows, and Carved Columns

Cows have grazed alongside humans for eons, and shaped us to be the people we are today. Their great weight has exerted a gravitational pull on the trajectories of our human cultures. Cattle and Humans are buddies who go *way* back! It's fascinating to follow the cow-trail back through history.

Aurochs & Lascaux: The Hall of the Bulls

The pyramids used to be the gold standard for archaeological knowledge of human beings. There are definitely cows in the pyramids. But our association started millennia before that.

Archaeologists scrambling around on their backs in a cave in Borneo found a big red cow. They published a paper on it in 2014, and reported that it was the oldest known picture of anything—at least 40,000 years old (Handwerk, 2018)! It's a wonderful cow! It's drawn in red ochre in the Rudolf-the-Red-Nosed-Reindeer pose, legs outstretched front and back in a very capable 3-D rendering. There are stenciled handprints all around, so we can see that the artist did not stint their precious pigment: the beast is five artist-hands from nose to tail, and three hands high. That's a lot of ochre to crush up and mix with fat and blood to turn it into paint. On its rearing head it has two vicious recurved horns.

This discovery shows two important things. One is that the popular art-school textbook concept that *Europe Was the Cradle of Pictorial Art* is actually a steaming pile of bovine excrement. Secondly, it proves that humans and cows have had a long intertwined history. Thirdly, it demonstrates that humans have been *admiring* cows for a long time. Of all the things that might have been our first known picture, it's a cow!

We find that people were sketching cows long before we even considered the cows of ancient Egyptian art. The awe-inspiring Hall of the Bulls at Lascaux provides a glorious stampede snapshot from about 17,000 years ago. And the carving of the slaughtered cow from Göbekli Tepe (with its tongue hanging out) brings us right up to 12,000 years ago, millennia before Stonehenge and the Pyramids. We have a deep connection with cows!

Dairy Deities? The Cult of the Cosmic Cow

The sacrificial bull at Göbekli Tepe leads us in, on a trail of blood, to the great Bovine Mysteries. Cows have been deified and sacrificed to deities, sometimes at the same time! The awareness of the awesome and incalculable power of a mighty bull compared to a puny person has often widened out to an infinite horizon. The Bull becomes the archetypical god-figure, and the human task becomes the pacifying of a reckless divinity in the form of an uncontrollable ungulate. With the way things can suddenly go catastrophically wrong in our "civilized" world, one can understand the explanation for our broken lives as being like the trail of destruction left by a rampaging bull.

On the positive side, in a world without steam or petrol driven engines, bullpower is the best for plowing, threshing, and transporting crops. It takes only a little leap of the imagination to move from an impressively powerful animal to an impressively powerful deity. Imagine how useful a really *big* bull would be!

It's only one little step from imagination to religion, and a class of priests emerging who enjoy eating sacrificial beef.

Bulls were a cornerstone of religion across the fertile crescent. They were depicted as *under* deities, *with* deities, *as* deities and sacrificed *to* deities. Their horns could be worked in as a handy design element of a crescent moon, if you were wanting to worship our satellite. The Egyptians, however, cranked it up a notch.

The Egyptians seem to have had a thing about cosmic cross-species blends. They certainly put cows into the mix. Their cosmic cow was known as Hathor, generally considered to be a nurturing, motherly sort of being, full of the milk of divine kindness, and ready to welcome a soul in need into the afterlife. Often portrayed as a white cow, Hathor was one of the nicest Egyptian deities. She was also quite a sexy cow, and was helpful in conceptions and pregnancies. In addition she was a musical cow… perhaps Egyptians had already noted how attractive cows find music!

And so it continues. Cows have lived alongside humans so closely that they have insinuated their unlikely ungulate bulk into many sacred spaces. The Chinese had a Spring Bull Piñata, where people beat dried clay off a wooden ox image with bamboo poles. The Chinese also honored the Cow by naming one of the years in their 12-year cycle the "year of the ox." Troops of Zulu warriors break a bull's neck by hand once a year. A Roman initiate into the religion of Mithras had to stand under a stone grating. A bull was then slaughtered on top of the grating and the candidate was drenched in the hot blood of the dying animal. Gary Larson couldn't make this stuff up!

Now that we are urbanized, though, we have forgotten the primal terror of the Bull. We no longer feel awed by cattle. Cows have become cute. Only the constellation of Taurus swings by silently in the sky to remind us of the former formidable force of the cow.

The First Cowboys: When Humans First Herded Cattle

At some point we put a ring on our relationship with the Cow, through its nose. Whoever the current self-appointed cow expert is over at Wikipedia assures us that we began domesticating cattle about 10,500 years ago in Turkey and Iran. By domesticate, I mean getting a cow to the point where instead of impaling you to the barn door, she lets you milk her peacefully. She doesn't even put her foot in the milk bucket.

Genetic studies indicate that this miracle of mutual accommodation emerged from a manic herd of about 80 wild aurochs (Science Daily, 2012). Aurochs have gone extinct as a species, but live on in their descendants, much like the dinosaurs live on in domestic chickens and ostriches. Apparently, some ancient Turkish or Iranianian hunters got tired of trekking after the wild herds and going horn-to-spear with these delicious monsters. Who knows how they got 80 of them penned up securely, though? And then somebody had the patience to separate out the smallest and meekest animals and get them to breed separately. Out of the calves produced by those *relatively* timid parents, they had to choose the (again, *relatively*) smaller and more amenable animals, and, following Gregor Mendel's principles, we reached the Domesticated Cow. Bully for us!

My favorite image from all our long years of shared landscape comes from about 4,000 years ago, from the tomb of a Middle Kingdom mummy. Egyptians loved to be buried with symbols of death and rebirth, and cows have featured in a few of them. The one I have in mind is an exquisite 22-cm-long painted wooden model (The Met, 2022). A man stands holding a white cow with black spots by a long-rotted string halter. The cow is in the process of giving birth to a calf, her tail twitched aside as the head and forelegs of the baby bovine emerge into the world of green grass. Another Egyptian stands ready to catch the calf. It is an astonishingly beautiful moment, captured for eternity and intended for none but the dead. I have ambivalent feelings about the nosey-parkerish attitude of archaeologists, but I am glad this little masterpiece is finally getting the recognition it deserves. Its message is clear. In life or death, from generation to generation, cows are our close companions!

Tollund Man's Hood and Ötzi the Iceman's Nice Leather Shoelaces

On May 6, 1950, the Jutland Crime Scene Investigators jolted out to a bizarre homicide near Tollund in the Bjældskovdal Bog, Denmark. Their Copenhagen-assembled Model A Ford jerked its way through the rutted Jutland "roads" and eventually arrived at where the visibly shaken family who had reported the incident were grouped around the gruesome cadaver. Somebody had recently attacked a man, strangled him with a plaited leather halter, and dumped him naked (except for a leather belt and leather cap) into the peat bog! Viggo, Emil and Grethe Hojgaard had been replenishing their peat stocks after a long winter when they came upon the shallow grave (Levine et al., 2017).

It turned out that this was not the work of crazed (contemporary) fetishists. The body was about 2,300 years old, and any witnesses to the murder of "Tollund Man" would be difficult to persuade to testify. The case was removed to the cold case files, and the archaeologists took over. High acidity, low oxygen, low temperatures, and chemicals in sphagnum moss—which produce such nice peat—had tanned and preserved his body and his leather restraint paraphernalia for two millenia. The archaeologists' best guess is that he was a sacrifice to the bog-god. My point here is this: leather lasts, and gives us many clues to our sometimes strange relationship with cowhide!

As an aside, it appears that antique Danes also used the peat bogs for storing that other wonderful cow-adjacent product, butter! Archaeologists occasionally come across forgotten prehistoric caches of greasy bread-spread in the bogs.

Another case in point, with regard to leather leaving taurine traces in history, is Ötzi the Iceman. Ötzi melted out of an Alpine glacier in 1991, having been kept in cryogenic perfection for about 5,200 years (Pinkowski, 2021). This tough 46-year-old mountaineer had been killed by an arrow, and all those millenia the ice has preserved the crime scene for our analysis. He had 61 tattoos and a copper ax. He wore an outfit made from various non-bovine leathers, a fur hat made from a brown bear, and cowhide shoelaces . Something about cowhide is apparently the right thing for fastening shoes. Archaeologists and paleo-leather experts have not yet solved the mystery!

Two-and-a-half millennia ago, a warrior was buried with a suit of tough rawhide scales in Northwest China (Geggel, 2022). Bits of cow leather tack show us how ancient Egyptians used to harness horses to their chariots. Roman legionaries conquered the barbaric Europeans on oxhide sandals. The Nguni tribes have used cowhide shields since time immemorial. In 2018 a 500-year-old skeleton was pulled out of the Thames still wearing his expensive boots, which tell as much about him as his deeply notched teeth (Baynes, 2018). The gigantic 2m-tall Old Croghan Man had a pretty plaited leather armband that somehow survived intact since the time of his burial in the last centuries of the Iron Age.

We have used leather from cows because it is flexible, tough, and durable. Objects made from leather have often weathered the attrition of time and brought us information from our earliest existence. In the fields of the deep past next to the cottages of our long-forgotten ancestors, cows were grazing.

Leather Leaves and Cowhide Covers

Cows have a place at the heart of our universities, a role in preserving and passing on the wisdom of the ages. This honor has not been earned by intellect, but by the durability of their skins. As the savage barbarians of Europe started shaving their beards shorter and aspiring after learning at the end of the Dark Ages, they encountered an obstacle. The Chinese were as reluctant to put paper on the world market as they were to publish the secrets of silk. And there was too much to remember!

Fortunately, the Church had a plan. The early Scriptures had all been scribbled on papyrus reed scrolls, but this did not do well in the damp Northern territories. There was already a functional alternative, however. From the second century BCE a Turkish invention had been making inroads into the world of literature: parchment, made from animal-skin scraped down to translucent sheets. The trade was centered at Pergamum. If the Apostle John's letter to Pergamum was written on papyrus, the answer almost certainly came back written on parchment. The parchment with the best reputation was made of calf-skin, scraped and stretched and scraped again until it was almost transparent. This came to be known as "vellum," a word derived from the Latin for—wait for it—calfskin.

By the end of the sixth century, all new knowledge in Egypt and Europe was being recorded on refined rawhide. Scrolls were abandoned, and the "codex" form of the book, with pages bound between leather or wooden covers, became the main memory chip of the ecclessial, academic, and political domains. Lots and lots of cows contributed to church documents and Papal Bulls, the preservation of dodgy history, and the keeping of undodgeable tax records. The Book of Kells is one notable example. The Domesday Book is another.

One fascinating example of this leather technology has been preserved, unsurprisingly, in a peat bog. The Faddan More Psalter was a leather-bound, vellum paged book with a lovely buttoned cover, and was pulled out of the bog in 2006, having been in the preserving brew for 1,200 years. Archaeologists are still delightedly puzzling over it. Perhaps it was tossed by some early Viking raider who thought that it wasn't enough leather to patch a sail.

Leather ruled. Eventually paper took over, though, and for centuries now we have lived amongst libraries of paper-paged and paper-backed codices. Interestingly, the day of the leather or paper codex is now drawing to a close. If you are reading this online, you are back to scrolling!

Chapter 3:

Consuming Cows and World Cultures—1,000 Ways to Eat a Cow

Before we deal with the leather we get from cows, I must deal with what comes inside the leather first. The leather industry can be seen as a byproduct of the beef industry. Or the other way round? It's one of those chicken/egg puzzles.

Whatever the case, the cow is almost universally popular on the menus of the world.

I remember visiting the wet market in Narathiwas, a small provincial town in South Thailand. If you veered counter-clockwise through the maze of stalls, you ended up at the Chinese pork stalls. But if you chose the Halaal clockwise sector, you would end up with the Beef Butchers. Each of their stalls would feature an entire beef carcass (at the start of the morning). As a shopper, you had to point to the part of the animal you wanted, and the butcher would remove a chunk roughly the right size for the price you were prepared to spend. Children growing up in such a context would never be under the illusion that supermarkets somehow created steak *ex nihilo*.

Thai people believe that it is seriously bad for your karmic profile to kill anything, and the larger the animal, the worse the karmic load is. Fish or crabs hardly count. But larger animals—pigs, cows, water buffaloes—they could much more credibly be believed to be reincarnated people. There is some good news on that front. According to some clever religious reasoning and fancy theological footwork, if you just come across a dead animal *that somebody else has killed*, there is no harm in eating a small bit of it. So technically the butcher gets the full blast of the karmic shotgun. He risks a few extra cycles of reincarnation for the good of society! Beef sales are brisk. The Thai do not eat a lot of animal protein, but they eat it in a lot of different dishes!

Roast Beef and the English Arteries

There was a time, in the 18th century, when the French dismissed the English as "*les Rosbifs,*" since roast beef was held to be so characteristic of the nation's tastes. There is some truth to this, as we British do love our roast beef and Yorkshire pudding Sunday dinners. In terms of our history, however, not all that much actual roast beef has been eaten by the workers of the nation. They have generally clogged their arteries with what are euphemistically called "the cheaper cuts." Sometimes they have had to be quite creative to make bits and bobs left over from the meat market palatable for a poor man's dinner. Here are a few highlights from the kitchens of the British.

1. Shepherd's Pie: Shepherd's Pie is made of that substance that hides within it all the mysteries of the butcher's day—beef mince, known in the United States as "ground beef." I guess that means that in some valley of North Yorkshire there must be a recipe for "Cowman's Pie" made with minced mutton, but I've never come across it. This is a chair recipe book, not a food recipe book, so all I will say is that you cook the mince and then cover it with a thick layer of mashed potato.

2. Tripe and onions: this cow product is not welcome in my home, although I quite like it. Tripe is the muscley skin of some part of the cow's digestive tract—the first stomach, the second stomach, the third stomach, or the last stomach. Salt it, soak it in vinegar, boil it in water, curry it, boil it in a white sauce, pack it with lots and lots of onions, and bake it. Despite all these culinary processes, most people still can't stomach it!

3. Haggis: The Scots are to blame for the haggis. It's mostly sheep innards and oats, but the true flavor is brought out by the fatty beef bits.

4. Faggots: The Welsh eat faggots. These are large "beef" mince meatballs held together with bovine stomach membrane. The Germans stopped the Welsh eating as many cows as they wanted during World War II, so they invented faggots to make sure no beef bits went to waste.

5. Brawn: You boil up a cow's feet with peppercorns and bay leaves, let it set in the fridge, and voila! Savory jelly you can slice and serve on toast!

6. Black pudding: Butchers mix oats or some other breakfast cereal in with the fresh blood, squeeze it into sausage skins, then slice it and fry it up for a fortifying morning snack, rich in iron. Often people don't fancy it for some reason.

Of course no survey of the beef-eating habits of the British can ignore the red-uniformed and red-faced guards of the Tower of London. They got their name "Beefeaters" when, as bodyguards for Henry VII, they were allowed to eat as much beef off the king's table as they liked. Cows shape culture in many mysterious ways.

Slabs of Steak and Mountains of Mince: The American Experience

You've heard of the American Dream, but did you ever wonder what it was? I have my suspicions that there is more to it than a home in the suburbs and a nine-to-five job. That dream includes eating great big walloping sizzling seasoned steaks—a dream about eating as many two-kilogram hunks of beef as possible.

Molly Schuyler, a mere 55kg in weight, is the unlikely steak-eating record holder. In 2014 she ate a 2kg steak in 2 minutes and 44 seconds! In 2015 she went on to eat three 2kg steaks in under 20 minutes (she started out on a fourth but unaccountably ran out of room). Molly is living the dream (Rocha, 2015)!

Americans eat a lot of beef. They emptied 21% of all cowskins in the world in 2020, thanks to their wealth and penchant for steak and burgers. China came in a distant second at 16%, followed closely by the EU and Brazil (Cook, 2022). The average American eats about 50kg of the juicy red stuff per year (Cook, 2022). The British might have the reputation for eating beef, but the gastronomic Olympians in the beef eating race are the American team!

American beef-eating cuisine is not characterized by subtlety. It's all about the volume. No little bite-sized strips or shaved curls of meat. It's generally either steak or hamburger, and usually massive steak and ponderous quarter-pounders.

The hamburger is a social phenomenon. Fried patties of ground beef (a.k.a. "hamburger" in the states, and known in Britain, conversely, as "mince") are stuffed into a bread roll along with salad stuff, sliced pickles, and high-carb sauces. Americans eat them everywhere, and export the culture to every part of the world they can. I had an American visit me once in Thailand, and with the vast and fascinating prospect of Thai food, he preferred to eat at McDonalds. Strange but true. It's probably got an entry in Ripley's *Believe It or Not*!

Dainty Eaters: How the Thai Eat the Least Possible Beef

The Thai have developed a peasant-derived beef menu that is quintessentially East Asian. The Thai generic word for "food" is "rice." Anything else is considered a spicy bonus. So when the Thai eat beef they are about the diametrically gastronomic opposite to the Americans. They chop things very small and add a lot of chillies before they cook their dishes. In a typical English kitchen, you cry when the onions go in. In a Thai kitchen, you cry and cough when the chopped chillies hit the hot oil!

There's one mouth-watering dish made from shreds of beef, basil, and rat-dropping chillies. There's another delicious rice additive that's made with chips of beef, marsh-spinach and rat-dropping chillies. There's a vegetarian vegetable dish only marred by the smallest amount of beef and rat-dropping chillies. There's the lovely late-night tripe soup (with rat-dropping chillies). And lastly (but not exhausting all the possibilities), there's the larp made out of raw minced beef, mint, and rat-dropping chillies. That last one is much favored by folk who have drunk too much and need a breakfast that will settle their stomachs.

So the Thai definitely *do* eat cows, but only in very small bites!

Wagyu: Marvelous Marbling on the Menu

Japan is tenth on the list of countries that have lots of leather lying around because they eat so much beef. Much could be said about the glories of Japanese beef dishes. I won't say it. But don't eat your Beef at an American Franchise next time you are in Tokyo. Try Nikujaga or Gyu Kushi, Beef Tataki or Yakiniku or Teppanyaki. Eat some melt-in-the-mouth Wagyu croquettes and Wagyu raw-beef sushi. Try those peasant bits and bobs treats that will not come at a price for a peasant's pocket: Gyutan (grilled sliced beef tongue) and Motsunabe (beef offal hot pot) (Gurunavi, 2017).

The myth is that the buttery-beef of the Japanese cow, the Wagyu ("wagyu" is Japanese for "Japanese cow"), is so expensive because cattle get fed beer and massaged daily. The story is that it takes such intense human-cow interaction to produce the astonishingly marbled beef that is characteristic of Japanese beef, 47.7% muscle and 41.7% fat. Wagyu cows are also bigger than average on the global cattle scale. However, it sadly turns out that the beer-and-massage regimen is all taurine turd. Japanese cows stand in fields and watch passers by like any other cows in the world. They are probably vaguely wondering whether anyone in the passing throng is likely to burst into song. Cows don't need to be massaged to get them relaxed—they were created relaxed.

Milk and Blood—Maasai Cattle

Beef consumption is tied to wealth. The wealthy still eat the cows that the poor care for. Africa is a continent of cattle, although only five of its countries make it into the top 50 beef-eating nations. The Nguni people love their cows, but they love them alive, not on the plate. The isiXhosa language has dozens of adjectives for describing cows, and herd boys can name and describe each of their charges. Rustling is extremely difficult amongst the amaXhosa because everybody knows which cows everybody else has. There are no anonymous herds to sneak a few extras into. The amaXhosa and other Nguni peoples do of course consume milk, most often in the form of the "African yogurt," *amasi*, traditionally created by pouring milk into designated leather *amasi* bags. Generations of bacteria turn the milk into a fizzy, sour, fermented drink, rather than allowing it to rot.

The Maasai of Kenya have a further way of feeding off cows without having to take off their hides. Traditionally, Maasai cattlemen will temporarily open a cow's vein and drain off about the same volume of blood as milk they have milked. This is mixed together in a sort of vampire's strawberry sundae, and it fuels the Maasai high energy lifestyle with a rich (but weirdly low-cholesterol inducing) diet. They consume *double the amount* of cholesterol recommended by the WHO, but they do not get heart disease. Many obese Westerners might want to swap genes, but then they would also have to swap their steaks for Kenyan pink milk.

La Vache Française: Cow-Eating in France

The best way to eat beef in France is to go to the same restaurant as often as you can afford, and work your way down the menu systematically. I doubt you *can* be disappointed! When you point to *"Alouettes sans têtes"* (which sound like headless birds but are not), you might not know what you are ordering, but you'll like it! You won't complain when they bring you your *"Beef bourguignon,"* either. Work your way steadily down the *carte*: *Châteaubriand*, *Entrecôte à la bordelaise*, *Gardiane de boeuf* (that's got beef in it, see), *Steak au poivre*, *Steak-frites* (which the Belgians helped the French create), *Tournedos à la bordelaise*, and *tournedos Rossini*. That's an itinerary for a week in the land of French beef. Unless, of course, you are Molly Schuyler. In which case you'll have to find something else to eat on day two.

You may wonder if there is a soft underbelly to French cuisine, a list of leftover recipes that the poor of the past had to eat (when they couldn't get any cake). Yes indeed! To an outsider they sound equally exotic, and of course these days they are equally expensive! When you point to *Tablier de Sapeur*, you will get a tasty dish of fried tripe in breadcrumbs. *Tripes à la mode de Caen* is a lip-smacking concoction of inter alia, tripe, ox-feet, and apple brandy, while *Foie de Veau à la Lyonnaise* will turn out to be good old liver and onions. Every culture finds a way to enjoy every bit of the cow!

Eating Cows in India?

80% of Indians in India are Hindu, and 1.7% are Sikh. They follow religions that are virulently opposed to the slaughter of cows, since cattle are considered either sacred or exempt from kitchen duty because of their value as beasts of burden. Only a small minority of Indians, the Muslims and Christians, enjoy the culinary savor of beef. And yet, India is fifth on the global list of beef eating nations (Cook, 2022). That is only because India has a population of a staggering

1.4Bn people, and even a tiny fraction of that can add up to a mountain of meat! In fact, India's *per capita* consumption of beef is extremely low.

If you can find a restaurant to serve it, the best Indian beef dish in my opinion is *Masala* curry. This savory dish has a well-deserved worldwide reputation, but is best enjoyed in its native habitat. Sellers of *Masala* curry in the West have come to realize that Western palates cannot cope with the real deal—at least, not the full amount of curry. Another British favorite is *Vindaloo*—which is actually unknown in India. It is purported to be from Goa, but it seems that it's really a fantasy-curry marketed by astute London-Indian merchants to cater for the late-night trade of drunken Brits desperate to sober up before reaching home.

A Thousand Ways to Eat a Cow

Humans have not only been influenced by cows since the sunny meadows of deep prehistory; they have also been given their actual shape by cows, amino-acid-molecule by amino-acid-molecule. We should always give credit where credit is due, and as a worker in leather, I want to pay proper tribute to the whole animal. We can sit on cows because we have already eaten them!

Chapter 4:

Besides Beef—Leather for the Leatherman

Once every last edible scrap of beef has been boiled, baked, roasted, and fried, there is still a great deal of value left on the table. Down the ages we humans have made extensive creative use of the bones and hides of these precious animals. The cow has turned grass into some of the most useful components of our innovative projects!

The Inner Reality of Cow Skin

It is probably never worth culling cattle just for their leather, but once you have cowhide in your hands, you are set to survive as a species.

Cows have the usual sort of skins that all mammals have, a three-layer sandwich of tough, protective cells, with a thick covering of hair. As in all mammals, this skin is the animal's largest organ, and a cowhide can get pretty big: on average we can get 1.8 x 1.2m of leather from a single cow. In order to preserve the skin, though, we have to first remove anything that might decompose, and we must preserve and enhance the proteins that are useful to us. The four fibrous proteins that make leather so valuable are the Marvel Comics-sounding quartet of reticulin, elastin, keratin, and collagen, which are all stretchy and tough. Once that skin is "cured," (meaning everything that might rot has been stripped out), we are left with a wonderful product. Leather flexes, folds, molds and holds: and it's tough as… leather!

The History of Herbivore Hide-Hacks

As an upholsterer, I am amazed at the versatility of leather. Cow skins are admirable not only for accommodating arses! Picking up from prehistory, cowhide has been used for an incredibly wide array of civilization-enhancing purposes, and the written record is full of leather!

Protective Equipment

There are many qualities in leather that make it ideal for protective applications. Leather is relatively light, but unlike other materials, it is a very tough substance. It does not puncture or catch fire easily, it absorbs quite heavy impacts without deformation, and is perfect for protecting against scrapes and scuffs. It is not by accident that leather is the archetypical shoe material. Down the ages, blacksmiths and farriers have sworn by their leather aprons. Once you are dealing with metal at over 1000°C you are going to be picky about protecting your tummy and toolkit. Leather cannot be used for every sort of protection, but it's a good friend when you need it!

Leather has been the go-to fabric for personal protection down the ages. The English archers who decimated the French iron-clad heavy cavalry with longbows at Agincourt each had an important piece of leather protection—the thumb guard. If you need something light and tough that will stop your bowstring skinning your thumb over a day of intensive archery, it must be leather.

Another group of skilled workmen who have plied their trade since the dark ages are the falconers. Many birds of the gauntlet can exert more than 200psi with the grip of their talons, easily enough to crack wrist-bones. Hence the gauntlet—a rugged leather glove that can make hunting rabbits a pleasure, rather than a penance.

Speaking of gloves and hot metal, welders' gloves are made from cow split leather, which are more than capable of protecting humans from sparks and droplets of molten metal. The baseball mitt is a specialist glove of another sort, and leather is still the preferred medium for making it. The mitt not only enables the fielders to endure multiple impacts, but also forms a sort of catching basket to improve their catching efficiency. Only the wicket keeper is allowed gloves in cricket, and the wickie's high-tech hand gear also relies on leather components. Cricketing fielders just have to make do with developing the toughness of their own leather. And before we go on from cricket, let us reflect on the importance of leather for making a cricket ball. There is much debate over the abrasion rate of Duke vs. Kookaburra balls.

Motorcycle leathers are the protective equipment that display the anti-abrasive quality of cowhide most dramatically. The motorcyclist loses it on the apex of turn five where he is just touching 180kmph. The bike goes down and slides across the asphalt and comes to a halt deep in the gravel. The rider goes down with the bike but gets peeled off by friction, and follows it across the asphalt and into the gravel. Then he stands up and kicks his bike! Why hasn't he been grated like parmesan cheese all over the racetrack? The answer lies in the miraculous resistance leather has to being scraped off. His boots, gloves, jacket, and trousers have kept him safe in a cocoon of cowhide.

Industrial Applications

When leather is not used for upholstery or protective gear, it finds many uses in industry. I remember the barber in my childhood, stropping his cut-throat razor on a leather strap. It seemed completely mysterious. It took me until my adult years—and finding a hipster barber—to discover that the strop is just rearranging atoms on the very thin edge of the blade. Apparently, in the process of shaving, the beard hairs bend the edge over slightly, and the leather strop straightens the edge out again!

A more heavy-duty use of leather is for the straps that drive machinery like lathes. Leather first took on this role at the beginning of the industrial revolution, when first horse-powered machinery, and then water and steam-powered rigs, required linkage between the primary rotating axle and the machines it was intended to power at a different speed. Pictures of Victorian factories show vast halls festooned with orderly leather spiderwebs, as the power from a spindle rotating near the ceiling was transferred by flywheels and straps to the machines of the workforce down below.

We can go back in time to the forge. The bellows used to bring the fire up to a high enough temperature to forge iron and steel have always depended on a material that doesn't wear out with repeated folding and unfolding. That could only be leather with its collagen and other flexible proteins. You can still often find leather bellows in forges.

Domestic Use

Leather found a thousand uses around the house in pre-industrial times. It could be whittled down fine and then, if need be, woven together to make a fastening cord of various weights. Leather coils also served as a poor man's hinge on doors and boxes, where once again its resistance to wearing out with repeated folding was an essential quality.

Leather is fairly waterproof, and can be made entirely so by a judicious application of neatsfoot oil (oil made from neat, i.e. cattle!). People have made cups and buckets from the stuff. Leather cups were called "bombards," and were popular with tavern keepers because drunken patrons could not readily break them. In the East leather was used for domestic water bottles and water bags (known from 3000 BCE as "mashaks," in a reference in the Rigveda).

And that which can contain water can contain wine. Wineskins could gently stretch with the fermenting gasses, and be conveniently carried around to where it was needed most. Long before amphorae, oak barrels, or glass bottles, the characteristic bouquet of a good wine would be "leathery" and the finish "cow-ish"!

Military Applications

Leather is quite slash and puncture-proof in itself, and the poor soldier's armor throughout history has often been a leather jacket, shield, and cap, all hardened by boiling. The more pieces of metal that could be hung on it, the more arrow-proof it became. But there was a drawback—if your gear got too heavy, you might become a sitting duck during close-quarter fighting. Perhaps I should say "sitting tortoise"? Leather was also a major component of the plate armor worn by wealthy soldiers on horseback. The plates and joints of the outfit had to be flexible enough to allow the man to fight, and that was achieved by leather straps and buckles. The whole fighting rig would be a jingly mass of steel hung on a web of leather strapping.

All that rattling and squeaking armor had to be hurled towards the enemy, and the transport of choice was the horse. Much could be written about horses, but I'm tracing the traces of the cow. Saddles and tack have always been leather. As an upholsterer, I recognize all the benefits of leather in the saddle, where so many people have sat on cows down the years. You can shape it, and it holds its shape. In this case, saddlers can mold the leather to both the horse's back and the rider's bum, so the cow becomes the horse-human interface. But it's flexible too, so it doesn't gall the horse's back or the human's balls. The tack is tough enough not to snap unexpectedly mid jump, or when the horse *really* doesn't want to do what the human wants—an important consideration when in the heat of battle.

All manner of military gear has made use of cow skin. Scabbards and belts, holsters and tents. One famous battle was won by a leather slingshot, but there are no records of what animal's skin it was made of. Humans are endlessly creative about inventing things to help kill others whilst defending themselves, and cows have been unwittingly drawn into that mayhem.

I have not caught every use for leather (for instance, I'm saving boots for later!). However, I would like to finish this section by discussing an important cow-related weapon of mass destruction. The bagpipes. These skirling sirens of the skirmish were created by bloodthirsty Northern British tribes who, to this day, use them to stir profound unease amongst their fellow islanders. Hadrian probably built his wall to keep the music of Scotland at bay, as much as anything. I cannot imagine a more martial use of leather. The leather is folded in half, and the two halves of the instrument are cut out together. It then passes through a series of mysterious processes involving shaping, cutting, and stitching, until it emerges as a battle-ready set of bagpipes. Take cover!

On the Farm

A lot of what we have discussed about military applications of leather applies to leather in agriculture too, where heavy loads are routinely shifted by large animals, and leather has been universally relied on to functionally attach animals to carts or plows or whatever. When it comes to transport, the whip has been crucial to keep things moving. It is not unusual for an ox to forget that it's supposed to be pulling a cart and decide that it wants to eat some of that grass. Snaffle bits not being suitable for cow control, the bullwhip is able to make its way through the thick hide of the animal to remind it of what it was supposed to be doing! Bullwhips are a work of art that deserve their own literature. We all remember Indiana Jones with appreciation.

Another place for leather on the farm are the chaps worn by cowboys. These are crotchless and footless waders made of leather, designed to protect the cowboy's legs from getting shredded by the cactus, mesquite, and sagebrush thorns they have to ride through. Puncture-proof leather is the way to go.

Sport, Leisure, and Cows

Here's a unique idea! Why not upholster a globe of high pressure air with a geometric patchwork of leather, and play a game kicking it around? About 700,000 official leather footballs are made each year, with one cowhide making about 20 balls. The NFL needs an entire convoy of trucks to bring all those hides to the football factories (Farr, 2021). Interestingly enough, the odd-shaped ball used in playing American football is also made of cow leather, despite being affectionately referred to as "pigskin." Rugby, golf, and hockey balls have gone the synthetic route, although they all started out as leather creations. Even as conservative a sport as polo has abandoned leather-covered cork for "high-impact plastic."

Hospitals and Hide

A little known fact about leather is that it is mildly antibacterial. It is also durable and cleanable, which has made it ideal for use in hospitals. Wheelchairs, arm restraints, and therapeutic furniture of all sorts have been traditionally upholstered in leather.

As an aside here, loads of medicines have some sort of cow product as an essential part of their makeup, even if not directly derived from their skins. Gelatin is used to manufacture capsules, an essential delivery system for unpleasant tasting concoctions. Insulin is derived from the cow pancreas. And if you read the fine print on the medicine bottle you were just prescribed, you will often find bovine traces.

From Four Feet to Two: Why Jimmy Choo Loves Cows

Fancy Footwear

The world of fashion leather needs exploration, too. Fashion designers are the upholsterers of the human frame, and at times they too use leather to work their wonders.

The history of how humans have worn hide goes back a long, long way.

The statues of the classical Greeks sometimes wear stone sandals. Those would have been leather in real life. The Egyptians had been wearing leather sandals in the desert for a long while already. We have some lovely examples of Egyptian shoes from various tombs, including a weird cache of seven shoes in a jar recently found tucked away in a temple. The jar preserved them nicely, but the shoe hoard consisted of three pairs of children's shoes and an arbitrary odd adult one (Jarus, 2013). They were the Jimmy Choos of their day, and we must assume they were a thief's cache—people who were corralled to move pyramid stones were limited to cheap woven papyrus footwear.

Since old footwear is as tough as old boots, shoes have survived quite nicely. There are Iron Age sandals and Viking leather boots. From more recent times, we have had monstrosities of fashion, such as the Crakow shoe with its long backward curled tip like a chameleon's tongue—a mark of high status in the court (Liberty Leather, 2021). A king or queen would have had a meter-long curlicue! It's a long road from a muddy meadow to a royal foot.

Leather footwear has taken a couple of interesting paths into the present. The workman's steel-toed boot is the descendent of the army boot. The football boot has stuck with leather, although the running shoe has begun to abandon it. It's the football boot, though, which has become the designer shoe of the sporting world—a high tech masterpiece of the cobbler's craft.

The other main shoe stream is the designer shoe and all the copies spawned by the industry. Jimmy Choo is the one designer who stands out for me: the son of a cobbler and a cobbler himself, who has turned cowhide into gold. He is much copied, supporting an entire industry of knockoffs that supply the demand from disapproving Italians that buy them in droves from Bangkok's MBK store.

Fabulous Fashion

Moving up the human frame from the feet, we find that leather from cows has an exciting reincarnation in the world of fashion. Dolce & Gabbana can take a piece of leather and turn it into something astonishing. Coco Chanel can cover your backside in a minidress in the latest style for a mere three grand, or barely cover your modesty for a paltry 4k. The transformation of the humble cow into such dizzying riches is a capitalist miracle!

But perhaps the most interesting wearers of leather are the Goths. Alaric the Goth and his brawny bandits who sacked Rome in 410 CE no doubt wore a lot of leather. However, nobody carries it off with such style and intensity as the contemporary Goth community. Gothic darkness is a fascinating cultural phenomenon, and has proved strangely durable, just like their black leather boots and spiky leather jackets.

Leather seems to do that to humans. Put it into human hands and they get inspired to use it to make their brightest and darkest dreams come true.

Chapter 5.

Dem Bones, Dem Bones, Dem Cow Bones

Why Waste Anything?

Now we have eaten all the edibles and used every scrap of the hide—what's left? A rather impressive 50kg pile of bones, and a bag of keratin hooves and horns.

Of Cows, Dogs, and Dynamite

Cow hooves are a classic dog treat. The vet has them in the equivalent of the shelf of sweeties and fizzy drinks (candies and sodas) at the till in the supermarket, tempting you to buy one last little treat for your dog. Dogs love disgusting things—so they are touchingly pleased at you offering them the keratin toenail of a cow! Fill one with peanut butter and your dog will gnaw on it under the table on a rainy day.

But canine pleasure is not the limit of the uses of the cow hoof. I don't know who first thought of it, but cow hooves are ground to powder to produce a keratin additive for fire extinguishers. It burns poorly, and boosts the effectiveness of the other components of what they call "viscoelastic polyurethane foams." Saved by the cow!

So much for *extinguishing* fires. If you are inclined to *start* one, specifically by using dramatic dynamite, you might be unaware that the cow is following you into your nefarious venture! Keratin powder from cow hooves (and feathers) is used to make the explosive safer to handle, and to get more bang for your buck. Slowing the explosion down can increase its power, for some mysterious alchemist's reason. While we are on the subject, dynamite manufacturers also use the glycerin from boiled down cow fat—that's why it's called nitro*glycerin*!

At the other end of the cow we have the horns. These can go into the same keratin mill as the hooves, but knife makers rather like them. Bladesmiths down the ages and across the continents have found that cow horns make excellent knife handles. The horn becomes malleable if you heat it to the right temperature, so you can shape it to a comfortable fit for the human hand. It is a tough and reliable way of interfacing your hand with a steel blade.

Movie Props to Jelly Tots

The premier use for cow bone is in the film industry. What western have you watched that doesn't have at least one sun-bleached steer skull nailed to a clapboard wall or the stump of a lightning-struck tree? I can imagine the props department out scouring the surrounding dessert for some suitably bleached bones for the next shot.

There are, however, many other less prominent but still very interesting applications for the cow skeleton. You might be eating cows more often than you think. There is an entire industry involved in boiling up cow bones to produce gelatin, and gelatin is an ingredient of many of our favorite foods. It's a complex process, but gelatin factories can turn cow bone into transparent, tasteless, and completely unsmellable gelatin. Various industries take it from there.

Industry also finds a use for a whole alphabet full of fatty acids that are melted out of bones. The chief one is stearic acid—or "steeric" acid, as I constantly miss-spell it, having cows on the brain these days.

Nice and neutral oily stuff is a key ingredient of cosmetics that require slipperiness. Lipstick has it, and so does soap. Toothpaste and shaving cream both sell better if they have that cow-fat feel. And that universal childhood cosmetic, the wax crayon, is oozing stearic acid as well.

Where would the sweets (candy) and dessert industries be without their vast vats of glycerin and stearic acid? Jelly *is* gelatin, it's right there in the name. Gummy bears are gummy because of gloopy cow by-products. That sugary "hang" or mouthfeel that keeps you buying stuff on impulse in the checkout queue at the supermarket (when you are not buying hooves at the vet) is produced by the hidden hoof of a cow.

Jet Fuel to Josiah Spode

Biofuels are one of the renewable resources that are touted as solutions for our global climate crisis. Many airlines are waving the biofuel banner as more and more clients frown at their carbon footprint. Apparently one can turn anything with carbohydrates into jet fuel, and cowbones deliver a lot of burnable potential. FedEx wants to obtain 30% of its fuel from sources like cow-bones, so the old rag 'n bone trade seems to be looking up (Swanson, 2015)!

Meanwhile, other industries have been quietly using a steady supply of cow bones. Have you ever come across the concept of "bone china"? It's not in vogue now, but when Josiah Spode first cut out the Chinese ceramic merchants with his exquisite translucent porcelain in the 1700s, he had discovered a magic ingredient. You do not want a bull in the china shop unless he's in the form of superfine bone-dust ash added to the clay. His crockery might still have been called "china," but British cowbones made the industry 100% British!

Heifers, Highways, and High-End Cars

A Jaguar XK has real leather everywhere you *see* it (seats, door panels, and dashboard). That's called a "full leather interior." Slightly downmarket versions of the X-Type Jag, however, apparently have "leather seating surfaces," and anything that doesn't actually come in contact with some part of a person is merely a synthetic substitute. But that does not end the Jaguar, or any other top-end automobile's association with the rural bovine: all its tires are stuffed full of stearic acid to keep them in shape, instead of melting after a while from constant friction. Plus, hydraulic brake fluid is made from cow bones, and even the asphalt on the roads uses oils extracted from beef bones to hold everything together!

We might be mostly urbanized these days, but we still use a lot of cow for a lot of stuff!

Fertilizer and Charcoal

There is another very impactful way in which to use cow bones: bone meal. If we grind up cowbones, we are left with a pile of Phosphorus-rich fertilizer. Plants only thrive if they have enough phosphorus to expand their root systems and do all that carbon-fixing and oxygen-producing photosynthesis. Plants desperately need phosphorus, and farmers and gardeners desperately want to feed it to them. The readiest source is our old friend the cow, once again. Bone meal is also rich in calcium. It basically *is* calcium. Grass (and other crops) will gratefully incorporate the calcium from cows' bones in their cell walls. Other cows will eat the grass and convert it into cow. The great cycle of nature rolls on!

All done? Not quite. Charcoal from burnt cow bone is used in the sort of steel that is used for making ball bearings. And the charcoal is also used as a very effective filter in the sweet industry. Against all probability, this black, grubby substance is used to filter and purify sugar, removing all impurities and resulting in a crystal clear product much favored by the confectionary trade.

Now I'm done!

The Future of the Cow Bone Industry?

Perhaps you are interested in beef futures? In the distant past, during the Shang Dynasty, a qualified Shaman would have made a prediction of stock movements for you, and would have inscribed his findings on the conveniently flat shoulder blade of an ox, the so-called "oracle bone." The oldest examples of Chinese writing have been preserved that way. Nowadays, you could take a Safari to South Africa and get a Sangoma to throw the bones for you in Soweto. And the "bones" she would roll out for you (on her oxhide) would largely be cow vertebrae (with the occasional domino, die, and hyena tooth).

Cows stick to our boots like cow dung we've trod on in a meadow. We cannot easily scrape off the traces of the journey we've traveled together.

Where There's Muck There's Money: The Value of Cow Poo

We've eaten all the meat. We've used every scrap of skin. We've boiled and ground every last morsel of useful product from the bones and hooves and horns. But there's still more! Believe it or not, the cow *still* has something very valuable left for us to exploit.

All the dung it has left behind it!

Throughout the poor countries of the world, cow dung has been used as fuel for cooking. If it's nice and dry, it burns down to very nice coals that provide a steady, even heat. An added bonus is that it discourages mosquitoes, which probably counts as a medical benefit. Mosquitoes are famously the most dangerous animal in Africa, as you probably know from your last pub quiz night. Many more people die from malaria and dengue than from the deadly tantrums of the hippopotamus (the second-most deadly killer).

Scientists are fascinated with ungulate excrement. It's got all sorts of microscopic critters that produce trace amounts of important chemicals. PhDs on cow poo are providing bedtime reading for dozens of readers worldwide. Cow pats are also a wonderful source of phosphorus, and generally an excellent booster for any weary patch of plants. In the right hands, cow poo turns to platinum!

And in Concowsion…

Cows march alongside humans in every aspect of our lives. We might have a sense of smell that is too delicate to tolerate a living, breathing, pooping cow too close to us. But the cow gets under our guard, and next thing we know it's lovingly licking our neck in a companionable way. Cows are real. Learn to like it!

Chapter 6:

Poo to Prada—the Stinky Skills of Curing Cowhide

Luscious leather is worth the putrid process that it has to go through to make it comfortable to use. So what happens? The cow doesn't just shrug off its coat and allow us to splash it over our living room floors for the chic look. If you take a good look at even your most natural-looking cowhide, you can see it's been through a lot of processes.

A Shout Out for the Traditional Tanners

These are the heroes of the leather industry, the hardy workmen who discovered that if you could endure the stench of the process, you could end up with this most versatile of materials.

Willows, Tea, and Tannin' Hides

For some odd reason, we enjoy drinking the chemical that is central to the *tanning* of hides—*tannin*. It's exactly this that gives tea its bitter tang, so beloved by billions of tea-drinkers. In fact, if you don't have any better use for them, tea leaves are an excellent medium for the natural tanning of leather. The peat bogs of Northern Europe are also full of natural tannin—which is one reason why human sacrifices from the dark ages have been so well preserved. It makes me wonder what the stomach of your average Briton looks like. After a lifetime of tea addiction, it must look like an old-fashioned leather football! On the other hand, coffee is not nearly as likely to preserve leather well. It has as much caffeine as tea, but way less tannin.

Left to itself, leather would just rot and fall apart. The miracle of tannins, though, is that they chemically bond with the collagens (decomposable proteins in the cow's hide) and cause a tough leatherization of the fibers. A finished, ready-to-use hide might contain as little as 8% tannin to as much as 45 % (ColourLock, 2022). The history of leather tanning has been the history of finding stuff that transforms cow skin into leather.

It took eons of experimentation. From leather's early obvious uses as a temporary rawhide string, it must have taken a lot of guesswork to find that soaking a bloody hide in a bucket of willow bark and water would make a better apron to cover your bum. Traditional sources of tannin have been olive leaves, walnuts, and Tara bushes. Tara comes from Peru, like Paddington Bear. It has a nice yellow flower, thorny stems, and a prodigious amount of tannin. It is grown worldwide as a source for tanneries. The word tannin itself seems to derive from the Latin for "oak tree," and the Old Cornish word "tann" meant red oak. To be fair, tannin is relatively common in plants. Even grape vines have tannin, although nobody in history has been known to tan cowhides in red wine.

But, I am getting ahead of myself. There are some steps to take before we get to the tanning tannin tea party.

Wrangling Raw Cowhide

The first thing to do with the cow's skin is to remove all traces of meat. In Neolithic times cavemen used to chip a certain shape of flint knife to do this particular job. As metals came into common use, the "fleshing knife" carried on with the shape. Still today, people who work with hides by hand use the same-shaped instruments as our earliest ancestors. Ancient leatherworkers used to pee on the hides at this point, or even soak the hides in vats of urine. Urine is a great way of loosening pieces of dried meat from a skin that had dried out, because it didn't quite get into the tanning process quickly enough. Helpfully, urine also comes out sterile and acidic, so it was the first step in fighting the rotting process. They could turn the toilets at major football stadiums into fantastic tannery projects, at 35,000l of urine per match!

Next, add salt. No salt bae sprinkle, but pack it on, completely covering the non-fur side. Fold the skin over and roll it up, and leave it for a day. Then, shake off the old salt and pack it with a new lot, fold it and roll it up, and cache for another day. It will now be quite oozy, and starting to smell bad. Keep the faith. This will come out okay! Then boil up as many liters of water as will cover your hide. Dissolve a couple of kilograms of salt in it and let it cool down. Dump the large soggy mass in, and weigh it down with rocks so that everything is covered. Leave it overnight to steep, unless you want to keep the hair on. In that case, haul it out at midnight.

Then, wash the hide thoroughly in soapy water, rinse it out well, and drape it over a clothes horse or fencing rail until it is only damp, and still malleable.

Now comes the tannin-rich tanning mixture, brewed as strong as possible. At this stage some tribes around the world rub in raw cow brains. Nothing smells good at this point. If you have the sort of sensitive nose that can detect the terroir of a wine, you really should not be doing this. A traditional and highly-effective element of your tanning mixture could be a slurry of rehydrated dried dog excrement and water. Massage the mixture deep into the leather, then fold it over on itself and leave it to stew overnight. After that, open it up and leave it indoors somewhere to dry slowly. Keep manipulating the hide every now and then to make sure it ends up being supple.

This is the point at which fights will start to break out in your apartment complex, due to the strangely divisive nature of the stench. Opinion is divided over how stinky leather is at this point. You think it's a bearable aroma. Your neighbors, on the other hand, think that the belly of hell has broken open and is pouring out suppurating demon guts. You should perhaps choose to do this farther away from human habitation!

In two or three days, the hide will be fully dry. Keep on stretching and pulling it over a low tree branch or a large boulder. After about a week of this you have a usable hide. And probably no more friends.

Technical Tanning: Sludgy Skin to Lovely Leather

I am not going to get too technical here, but there is a sort of grisly fascination in putting on wellies and a hooded waterproof jacket and visiting the guts of the leather trade. If you are going to work in leather upholstery ethically, you need to be at peace with the entire process, not just limiting your knowledge to the floor of the fragrant leather warehouse.

I remember my first visit to a tannery—distressingly clearly. I was working as a designer for Christie Tyler, one of the largest upholstery manufacturing groups in the EU at the time. I organized a site tour of a tannery for myself, but planned it poorly. The night before, I supped somewhat freely on red wine and limoncello, perfect accompaniments for a lovely *pasta con pomodoro e basilico*, followed by a luscious *tiramisu*.

When I woke up the next morning, I was fairly well hungover, with an eye-squinting headache and a little queasy in my stomach. *That's fine*, I thought. *I'll just eat a lot of toast for breakfast to mop up my system.* I had heard it was a fairly noxious environment at the tannery. It was.

The smell started to threaten me as I parked my car. As I met my guide, it worsened. "You get used to the smell," he said, with a wry glance at the pallor behind my sunglasses and my sweaty forehead. We walked down an alley where a workman was cleaning the pavement with a high-pressure water hose. The building ahead was grumbling with heavy machinery. We went in the truck-sized front door.

I had thought the smell could not get much worse. How wrong I was.

I had stepped into a vast hall where titanic, roof-high washing machines were churning gloopy masses of cowhides with a monstrous slurping and slapping. The smell became suffocating. Everywhere there were oozing crates of sloppy processed leather, the notorious "wet blue." Everything was a crashing pandemonium of mighty machines, with slimy hides and chemicals flavoring the air.

My stomach churned and a paroxysm of nausea engulfed me.

I lost 800 grams of fine Italian dining in less than two minutes, and added microscopically to the all-encompassing stench!

Beamhouse Operations

Let's start at the beginning. In the old days the raw hides used to be delivered to the "Beamhouse," where skilled workers would drape the hides over a wide, rounded beam and scrape them clean, as per step one in my tanning-by-hand instructions above. All these first processes are now done mechanically, but we remember the powerful men who used to do this work by the name we continue to use.

There are several key stages and I have personally experienced them in many different places and countries. The whole process starts with soaking the hides in vast vats, which cleans them off and gets them ready for step two, liming. Machinery adds lime and agitates the hides to remove all the hair and the inner parts of the skins. Machines then complete that process, after which the hides are delimed again by adding acids. Enzymes are then added to soften the wet hides in a process called "bating," and then the hides are pickled. This sounds tasty, but does not smell too good. In effect, pickling is adding lots of salt and other acids.

The hides are then split by machine into the expensive outside layer, which has the nice leather "look" and is much stronger, and the cheaper inner suede layer. Then comes the actual "tanning" using chrome and/or other chemicals to complete the transformation from skin to leather. Lastly, the leather is squeezed out until half the moisture is removed, and we are left with the proto-leather called "wet blue" (which, as we have seen, is sometimes wet with limoncello as well as water).

Finding a Tannery Near You!

Of course you now want to share my experiences! Just go easy on the limoncello the night before, or ensure there's plenty of crates to lose weight behind!

Well, if you are in China, you'll find a tannery easily, because China processed 40% of the world's bovine skin in 2020. Coronavirus played old Harry with the leather industry too, so more recent statistics are too depressing to mention. COVID-19 sucker-punched the global hide market, and as I write this, the demand for leather is only just recovering, so figures from before the pandemic are a better guide to what usually happens (BizVibe, 2020). The second easiest country to find a tannery will be Brazil, with its 2.4Bn square feet of leather per annum, which would be enough to carpet the whole of Heathrow airport, and a lot of the runway. That is followed by Russia and "other top leather producers" (BizVibe, 2020)—countries like Italy, Argentina and the USA. Fascinatingly enough, India, with its religious respect for the cow, is nonetheless right up there in the top ten.

Anyway, you have two options to find your first tannery. Google it and follow Google Maps directions; or just follow your nose! It's hard to hide the presence of a tannery. I have a friend who, as a child, used to take part in an annual schools' athletics event near a tannery. When it was originally built, the tannery was on the distant outskirts of the city. But the city had grown up around it, and property and rental prices for premises near it were very low. Eventually it closed operations, sold out, and is now a hipster business park called "Tannery Park." Few people can remember its former olfactory glory.

An Aldehyde-to-Zeolite of Tanning Options

The classic compound, as we have discussed, is tannin. This was the go-to chemical since humans first started herding cows and curing hides. It just *worked*.

In the 1850s, though, a remarkable advance in the process was discovered. Chromium sulfate salts produced leather out of cow skin in 24 hours! Before that, it would take about three months of soaking in tannin solutions. Efficiency was the name of the game, and soon there was more than enough leather to keep all those Victorian factories supplied with pulley belts. Still today most leather is processed this way (Carl Friedrik, 2021). It's quick and nasty. Unfortunately, nobody could smell the nastiness of chrome salts. Chrome is a heavy metal. It persists in ecosystems over time, and unregulated effluent from tanneries can have disastrous repercussions on the wildlife downstream. Gradually, public opinion is pressuring the industry to change, and some ingenuity is being put into alternative processes. The leather industry is quick to point out that they use *trivalent* chromium, which is non-carcinogenic (unlike *hexavalent* chrome, which is). Yet, the damage to the environment due to unregulated effluent in less-well-regulated parts of the world is undeniable (Nera Tanning, 2020). The reputational damage is becoming too extreme, whatever the merits of the chemists' debate, and the industry is trying to move away from chrome altogether.

The prize is a natural product (like tannin) that will not leave an indelible mark on the planet. Aldehydes show promise by offering a better resistance to water and sweat than chrome-tanned leather. But, overall they don't quite get the job done like chrome. Aldehydes are poisonous, for one thing. Lots of very "natural" things *are* poisonous, and it's easier to clean up effluent from Aldehyde usage. Fortunately, the engine of profitability is now slowly allowing the release of research funding to get scientists working out how aldehydes might replace chrome (Chen et al., 2021).

More promising than aldehydes, however, is what is known as "zeology." It looks as if this option is going to be able to deliver a "green" product, confusingly called "Zeo White." In terms of the product itself, Zeo White tanned leather has a nice tight grain, doesn't fade in the light, and is tough and heat resistant. So to put it all together, Zeo White wet blue is green! All we need now is for established tanneries to take a break in production and convert (Nera Tanning, 2020). But we all know that the politics of suppliers and pressure of demand is going to make that a slow process. The option is there, though, to ditch chrome for the first time since it was introduced.

Nothing can be done about the smell, though!

Chapter 7:

Training in the Tricks of the Trade

Leather furniture is one of the very few mass-made items that is still handmade. True, one needs a heavy-duty sewing machine to put everything together. Every piece of leather furniture, though, has to be cut out and assembled by a human being. There is no robot (yet!) that can perform the intuitive work required to clad a sofa or chair with slightly unpredictable leather.

So far, I have spent my career learning how upholstery works and designing leather furniture. There is a lot to learn about unlocking leather's incredible potential. Before I could get a toehold in the industry, though, I first had to go to university to learn the fundamental principles of upholstery design theory!

I had to learn *how* to learn.

University Days

First up, I had to rack up the mandatory student debt, spending everything that remained after paying my fees on ropey accommodation and cheap beer. I lubricated my study of upholstery basics with a high-alcohol and trans-fat diet.

My fees for the Birmingham Institute of Art and Design were not cheap. I felt in my bones, though, that this was where my obscure fascination with furniture was going to morph into a professional career. It was worth the investment. I come from a very musical family, but I was convinced I should take some tentative steps to branch out from the auditory into the sensory.

I wanted everyone to share my delight of sitting on cows!

I sparred with my tutors—like every young bull, I needed to try out my strength on the herd leader! I was pushed by both their knowledge and their opinions. I was already too invested in my art to simply allow education to roll over me, only for me to emerge as a mass-produced graduate. I wrestled with the projects and opinions like an upholsterer has to wrestle that one last corner of a cushion cover into place. I rolled with the punches of evaluations of my work that I disagreed with. And the net result was that I emerged from the education process with that most useful of accomplishments—the ability to learn for myself.

My tutors must have heaved a sigh of relief when I left, although perhaps they felt a touch of pride, too. They had managed to wrangle this rowdy young bull through the gates of the BA bullpen! As part of my final major project, I elected to study people's seating habits. This might sound technical, but to give you some idea of what sort of student I was, I need to explain my research topic: "an eye for sensuous proportion." All I actually ended up doing was taking photos of my girlfriend sitting on a sofa in varying poses on a Sunday afternoon. Even at that stage I had an eye for sensuous design. I hoped that her short skirt would attract—and distract—the tutors from the complete lack of any comprehensive research and up my grade! It didn't work. It was judged to be "too generalized," and I was sent off to rewrite an in-depth investigation into ergonomics. Perhaps the only reason I was allowed a rewrite was because the "distraction" had worked its magic!

Pendragon, Wales, and Luscious Leather Loungewear

I owe my start in the upholstery business to the design director who spotted some potential in me as a fresh new graduate from uni. I remember the interview process clearly, the nervous submission of my *jejune* portfolio, the anxious wait to be interviewed, and then the anxious wait to be contacted again. The brave company that first hired me was the well-established Welsh firm of Pendragon, an old-school upholstery firm that rarely opened its doors to new young talent. I was lucky to be offered the job of "design assistant," and my career was launched.

The Pendragon Furniture Company was located in sunny Bridgend, South Wales, famous for having the largest housing estate in Europe, called Breckla. I lived there, handily close to my work in a cozy rented house. Bridgend is a place so famous for its cloudy fogginess that it had been selected as the ideal location for a WWII munitions storage depot. It was one of those spots in Great Britain the Luftwaffe Bombers were least likely to locate!

How shall I describe Bridgend? It's gray. The grass is green, on the other hand, the sheep are white, and vitamin D deficiency is at a national high. The clouds are gray. It rains a lot. Did I mention that it was gray? But it was in this cul-de-sac of arts and culture that I came into my own with furniture design, and first started catering for the insatiable human craving to sit on cows.

To be honest, I had somewhat exaggerated my good qualities in the interview. I had been so eloquent about my potential, and sketched so vividly the value I could bring to the company if only I were given the opportunity. Looking back now, I imagine that the design director had heard it all before. But he recognized some promise in me, and now here I was, stepping through the doors on the first day of my first professional workplace.

It was a gulp moment.

I had talked the talk; now I had to walk the walk.

The key strategy I had adopted for my interview was that I could make up for my complete lack of experience by being extremely ready to learn. I painted myself as Mr. Adept-at-Adaptation! Now here I was walking into a specialist leather upholstery business with zero knowledge of leather upholstery. The proof of the adaptability pie was in the adopting!

There was nothing to do but walk straight forward in the course I had chosen. During the onboarding process I requested time in each department of the manufacturing process, so as to "improve" (i.e. *acquire*) my knowledge. It was a request made out of bravado and a desire to impress my new employer, but as it turned out, it was one of my best early decisions.

I made a whole bunch of new friends across every level of the company as I bumbled into their departments and said things like "What's this?" and "Where do you poke this thing?" Also, I genuinely *did* want to understand and learn about upholstery. I had maybe overstated my value to the company in my interview, but my love of upholstery was genuine, down to the bone.

My new friends inducted me into all the secrets of their trade, including their secret language, upholsterers' slang. Working skin-on-skin all the time leaves its mark on upholsterers, and the sensuousness of their calling rubs off on their vocabulary. A truly comfortable sofa leaving the floor was praised by saying, "It sits like a bucket of tits"—i.e. it had an overwhelming sensation of softness and comfort. Somebody who drove a very hard bargain in the upholstery trade is "harder than a witches tit." Besides being initiated into new ways of speaking, however, I *did* pick up on all the essential methods of turning cows into sofas.

The *Other* Leather Smell

By the time that leather comes into the upholsterer's hands, a complete transformation has taken place. The stench of the tannery gives way to one of the most fragrant and comforting aromas on this planet. When I first visited Pendragon and first walked through the doors, I was immediately ravished by the fragrance of leather—unforgettably distinctive with the very essence of workmen and tools. It had quiet elements of sandalwood spice and oil, a woody aroma: the quintessential perfume of upholstery.

Chrome somewhat suppresses this natural pleasure, and car manufacturers are okay with that. They want to be able to deliver their new cars to customers with that sought after "new car" smell. You can get a tin of that smell, by the way, and spray it into your old Golf to make it smell like a new Porsche. Different leathers, tanned and finished using different methods, each have a unique olfactory signature. If you are good with wines you can probably get good with leathers too (just stay away from tanneries!). I began to realize, as a young upholstery designer, what a privilege it was to work with this marvelous substance.

In my early journeys through the departments at Pendragon, my favorite department was Leather Stores. This was a large industrial hall lined end to end with "leather horses," metal frames with rounded tops on which batches of leather were draped. The leather horses would be covered many hides deep, leather in all kinds of finish, soft supple leathers in every color and every different textural effect, each characterized by its own sensory individuality—stacked and stored accordingly. Experiencing all these nuances in leather was complemented by the unique olfactory aura of each individual finish.

I found the concentrated aroma of this place dizzyingly inspiring.

I felt like a Hobbit in a dragon's hoard. The cheapest single hide kept in there was still expensive. The highest grade hides had *astronomical* value. Millions of pound's worth of leather was just draped casually over stands for anybody to caress and inhale its "nose," as the wine-buffs say. The pulsation of wealth was so awesome it made me dizzy.

My continuing hands-on postgraduate training in leather upholstery taught me that to truly appreciate (and accurately value) the leather you choose to use, you must be able to expertly identify and judge a range of variables.

- Tanning method: Is this a standard chrome-tanned hide, a new zeolite tanned hide, or something you are not sure of (ask the foreman—he's the real expert !)?

- Leather part: The most expensive cut of leather is called (predictably) the number one cut. It comes from the small of the cow's back and constitutes about 13% of the cow's hide. The number two cut includes the number one cut area, and stretches from tail to shoulder, and down to in line with the udder. The next level down includes the others, but extends from the hock across to the chest, and up to the withers. The fourth cut is the belly and neck. If you need a large piece of leather for your project, you will need to know what compromises to make when including leather from several of these cut areas.

- Finishing: Here you are choosing with your final user in mind. Are you wanting a sharp electric color, or an old brown cow feel? The Leather Stores can provide you with anything you want, so you must consider the right direction.

- Intended use of the leather: You need to learn how to feel the edge of a hide and be able to decide whether this is destined for a designer couch or for cowhide camp stools. Upholsterers judge hides the way diamond dealers judge diamonds.

Blemished and Unblemished: Lifetime Marks a Cow

Cows are living, breathing animals, and their hides often show the marks of a happy lifetime of hustling with the herd. They bump and scrape and poke holes in each other with their horns. They pick up parasites, and their little scars can tell the story of their lives. The leather industry notes these little "blemishes" and ruthlessly eliminates them! It turns out that we really like sitting on cows—but we don't like the idea of them having had a life. For me that feels like disrespect, which is why I'm filling you in on the bovine backstory.

Before a hide is draped on a leather horse in Leather Stores, it goes through a rather stringent quality control process, where deeply experienced sorters squint at it carefully and pick up any "flaws."

To start with, the hide is fed through a machine to decide whether or not the tannery has given us as much leather as we paid for. The machine calculates the square inch area of the hide with lasers. Then you know exactly what you've got. It is important not to pay for the hide of a fat cow and then end up with the hide of a skinny cow. Leather is so expensive that small margins of error in hide size can result in significant impact on profits.

The recently deceased is then graded on the quality of its skin. An eagle-eyed evaluator makes a crime-scene chalk mark around any insect bites, scars or blemishes. Many pests leave their mark on a cow: ticks, mites, cattle grubs, flies, ticks, and lice all cause natural marks. Of course, the more Ivermectin the farmer has used, the fewer of these there will be! If the hide has been too insect infested, though, it will have to be tossed out—not for lack of utility, but simply for the look of it.

Other undesirable mementos of an eventful life are branding marks, cesarean scars, and barbed wire tears. They need to be cut out or disguised. We have found ingenious ways to tan, finish and fill these little discrepancies, allowing our picky public to not have to face the former lives of the cows which they buy to sit on.

There is more to it than simply nature-denying aesthetics here, though. Scars don't pull evenly. If you stretch some leather tightly over a shape, the scar area, lacking in colloidal stretchiness, slacks a little, so that the surface may not appear completely even. There is some practicality to not wanting to upholster with a duffed-up, bug-bitten herbivore hide.

Then comes the Hogwarts sorting hat moment of the leather industry: the hide is assigned a place on a high-piled leather horse, along with a heavy assortment of equivalent hides.

Experiences of an Appy Upholstery Designer

So we have colored it, softened it, scrutinized it for spots, and stacked it. This has just been the beginning of bovine reincarnation. Our cow is about to be repurposed and reformed—we will reshape our once earth-plodding pal into a sofa.

Of Chainmail and Leather Cutters

I first found out about the leather cutters in my early days at Pendragon. None of the career fairs I had ever been to had mentioned this job. It looked at first like a fairly simple occupation, and their pay seemed to be out of proportion to what they were required to do. I was missing important information!

Leather cutters are given a set of plastic templates that represent the different parts of a sofa. They set these out on relevant areas of the cow hide and cut out the shapes. It all seemed quite straightforward. With a knife in one hand and a chainmail metal glove on the other, they cut around templates all day long talking about football, fishing, and Friday nights out. That's it. No gophering about for bosses. No unpaid overtime. No student loans to repay.

Don't be deceived. It's harder than it looks. A skilled cutter—and these are very skilled people—can analyze around 55sq feet of hide within moments. Then they can unerringly apply templates in a complex Tetris puzzle, with different optimal positionings for the slightly different shapes of each hide. It isn't only about getting the most pieces out of any one hide. They also have to ensure that only the best parts are visible once the cow morphs into a sofa. A leather cutter does this many times in a day, and always seems to get it right. "Think twice and cut once," the tailors of Savile Row say, and there certainly is no better example of this than with these guys. They do the "thinking twice" bit lightning-fast, though, and have honed their art until it's as sharp as their knives. It was fascinating to watch.

They are a hard-headed lot—they can ingest seven pints of lager and a portion of mayonnaise chips in the evening and be slicing through cow skin with razor-sharp knives at seven the next morning with no apparent hesitation. Although, the most experienced cutters among them do have a distinct lack of digits on one hand, which makes them look like Welsh pirates!

Stitching Up

Carts laden with cut pieces are then moved in a steady stream to the sewing room. They are impatiently received here by an army of highly qualified machinists, who unload the carts and turn the puzzle pieces into sofa skins.

When I first visited this space I was shocked to see that they were patrolled by Quality Assurance personnel with hand-held metal detectors. I thought at first they were scanning the machinists for skivs and blades! Was I about to enter the roughest yard there was? It turned out, however, that it was *broken needles* QA was scanning for. It's common for needles to snap, and the leather furniture industry likes to guard its customers' derrieres from accidental puncture wounds. It's often the small things in life that matter most!

Sewing leather is enormously difficult—for starters leather is very dense, and when sewn together on top of itself can form a very thick, tough layer. Machinists have to pound the leather with leather mallets and shave parts off to thin out connecting areas that are too bulky to fit under the sewing machine heads. Also, anyone that has tried sewing leather knows that the machine pulls your work through and you have to keep up with it using your hands to guide it through very closely to an incredibly sharp and treacherously fast needle—not for the faint hearted or the easily distracted! Veteran machinists don't lose fingers, but they do have battle hardened hands! Every scar tells of little momentary lapses of attention on the path to becoming a master machinist.

I was on a mission to learn all about the process. There are different *threads*, I found, for different applications—different in what they are made of, as well as how thick they are. Different tasks sometimes call for different *needles*, and there are different sewing techniques, depending on how much strain a seam has to take, or whether or not it can be seen. Machinists have to do everything perfectly at high speed, like Formula 1 drivers.

Sofa Stuffing

Then came the final pulling and massaging of the sewn panels into place over the wood and foam frame. There is something immensely satisfying pulling sewn leather panels over a sofa frame and snuggly massaging it into its new form, stretching and tacking off areas, and giving the chair or sofa its final form. It is extremely physical getting the different elements—the frame, the foam, and the leather—to combine with sensuous synergy into a piece of luxury furniture. The leather resists and then surrenders, and the transformation is complete. The cow has become a couch.

But that is not the end, not quite yet. Before the newly created piece of furniture is allowed into the showroom, it undergoes intense scrutiny. Are you soft enough? Are you firm enough? Did we form you well? Are you fashionable and desirable? Are you the right shape for the right person at the right time? Are you ready to launch into your next life and last a hundred years?

As a designer and an inveterate user of leather in upholstery, I have a super soft spot for the unsung ungulate. I have relied so heavily on this medium for much of my creativity that I want to celebrate every aspect of this wonderful animal—especially its wonderful skin. As more and more people come to share my love for leather, I carry a simple mandate as a designer: to respect the material and to maximize its potential in any way I possibly can.

The Hallmarks of Great Leather Upholstery

The perfect leather-upholstered piece of furniture is all about the proportion and balance of materials. A finely judged equilibrium of finish and form creates a microsystem that engulfs and relaxes the person who sits on the upholstered piece, the sittee on the settee. You don't sit *on* leather as much as sink *into* it.

Over the years I've developed a profound grasp of buttock technology. My photography of girlfriends in short skirts ceased a long while back at uni! However, I still have an undimmed fascination with how people sit on and use upholstery. Sitting is one of my favorite positions, second only to the horizontal one. It took our human race many generations to become fully upright, and we were spurred into that by our need to chase after proto-cattle with sharp sticks. When we caught one, we ate it and took its skin to make things, and next thing we knew, we were making leather furniture. Ever since those days, we have been learning how to recline comfortably. Until today, where some dedicated humans have developed *connoisseur derrieres*.

Great leather-seating experiences open up for us in many places, and we can find great leather upholstery everywhere. We are not surprised that leather can morph and mold to our contours no matter what our mood or activity. We crave those leather car seats that feel like they are holding us in an extra protective hand. We work so much better in an ergonomically designed leather office chair, swinging and cradling us in its firm embrace. Our leather-upholstered dining chairs add an extra sensory experience to the meals we share. And everybody loves to simply kick back, slump down, and relax on their leather sofa when they reach the sanctity of their home.

As an upholstery designer and artist, leather upholstery is my favorite genre. There is no other space as dynamic as our domestic environment, and it demands a versatile piece of furniture. We can lie on our sofa cow, or drape ourselves over an arm, or lie on the floor with our feet on the seat. No furniture in a public space has the same creative uses. The leather sofa becomes our life companion. It really knows who we are, and always enjoys our company. Providing people with sofas is a wonderful reward in itself.

An essential characteristic of the great leather upholstery is versatility. We can argue about ergonomics and theorize about the "perfect articulation of the vertebral column." But that does not solve the problem that the upholstered product has to be comfortable for all people of all different shapes and sizes, accommodating an infinite variety of habitual seating habits. So I don't think my second college essay on the ergonomics of seating habits would have been much use in the real world of cow-sitting humans. Scientific research will never be able to account for the way people are going to want to use the product.

So, is it possible to make the perfect piece of leather-upholstered furniture for somebody to relax on, kicking back their feet and curling their coccyx and spine into the relaxing S-shape so discouraged by orthopedic surgeons? The leather-upholstered piece is perfect for everyone because it flexes into everybody's shape. And what more could you ask for a seating surface to relax on while you binge watch *Game of Thrones*? It *feels* so good, and what feels good can't be bad! Leather upholstery exudes the individuality of its unique origins, and versatility to provide comfort for all who come to it for seating.

The leather seating experience I'm looking for as I send my creations out into the world is that I want people to feel the leather supporting them *and* enveloping them. I want them to experience what I experience. I like to connect directly with leather. It is an incredible substance which links me back with my earliest forefathers. Its durability secures and reassures me, and the skin-on-skin touch of leather on the back of my neck and hands and feet is soothing and relaxing. I want those who end up owning my creations to experience how this sensational material warms or cools to our environment. I want them to enjoy how it ages companionably alongside them, sharing their resilience and memory over the years.

The perfect leather-upholstered piece of furniture will age well, as time-resistant as leather itself. In a well designed piece made of good leather, its tactile steadfastness will become an essential part of the owner's life, and the patina of use will shine through reassuringly the more it is sat upon.

Chapter 8:

Seeking Hide—Selecting Leather

I have been to leather fairs all over the world, from Shanghai to Milan. As my career and expertise developed and my responsibility as a designer to meet my clients' needs expanded, I had to investigate wider possibilities for leather upholstery. Running a global upholstery furniture design studio that draws clients from all over the world, I am completely responsible for finding the newest-looking finishes and best leather from the right cow. From leather chairs to beds, and everything in between, I have to meet my clients' requirements using the best materials available.

Spoiler alert: I am now going to spill some leather industry secrets!

The Split Personality of Commercial Leather: Leather and Leather Split

By now you will have realized that you can't just order a container of "tanned cow skin." Not all leathers are created equal. You need to touch the goods before you buy them.

Hide: Layer upon Layer upon Layer

Firstly, we get a lot of different grades of leather from the same cow. We use huge mechanized band saws to separate the thick hide into thin layers—full grain/top grain, and "split," which can be processed into "corrected grain." And then there is the ghost of the cutting floor: bonded leather.

- *Full grain leather* is the most expensive, showing the natural grains and skin patterns. Look carefully though, because

- *top grain* leather is also outer leather, but it has had its outermost layer skimmed off and had blemishes sanded away, and then it's been recolored. Be careful, though, to distinguish it from

- *corrected grain leather*, which is the suede, or inner layer of the hide. This is not as durable or as quality as the top part, as it is less elastic and less tough. It is either used as it is, or transformed into a faux full grain look by compressing it with heavy machinery, after which a nice full grain pattern is rolled back onto the surface. This is labeled, euphemistically but honestly, "genuine leather." This is not, however, the bottom of the pile yet. The lowest leather is

- *bonded leather*, which is "mostly leather." It is the composition board of the leather industry, and consists of all the scraps chopped up finely and then bonded together with glue in useful sheets. Then the old trick of stamping a faux grain is perpetrated on the customer. *Caveat emptor*, as they said in Rome—let the buyer beware!

Splitting Hairs over Hides

Canny buyers may have noticed that for some time leather upholstery has been marketed in many varying ways—leather and leather split, leather match, full leather facing, etc. With the best options, you'll be receiving leather of some sort all over. Lesser examples of the upholsterer's craft will see half of your sofa consisting of very well made PU's that have been ingeniously integrated so that you might not notice. The leather devil is in the details.

The reason that chainmail-clad leather cutters get paid the big bucks is that they understand the game. In order to reach price targets, they need to ensure that furniture gets upholstered with top grain leather in areas of most wearability, and with split in areas of less sitting stress (and in places where it won't be seen). This results in significant savings and significant profits. And the object is bona fide, genuine, all-the-way-through leather, right?

The retailer's game extends its hidden hand into, um, *creatively describing* leather furniture. Here's what to look out for in the commercial world of upholstery, a sample of the perfectly true things your serious and enthusiastic sales person might say:

- "*Leather match/half leather.*" From slightly down-from-the-top luxury car seats to the offices of lower-than-chief executives, leather match is the way of acquiring the luxury of leather at lower cost. You must know that a product labeled "leather seating" will be leather anywhere a human might touch it, but the side panels and back will be made of a leather-lookalike. It's a very good imitation, though. But if you need to know, ask about it!

- "*Leather split.*" This is the under-layer of the hide. Its disadvantage is that it does not have the same toughness as top layer leathers, and so must be used for applications where there is no stress to tear it. Its advantage is that it is undeniably also leather, and as such is technically referred to as "genuine leather" with a straight face.

- "*Leather look.*" This is stamped, bonded leather that looks cool, but will not last. It is also much cheaper, though, so you need to do a swings-roundabouts assessment. It is also unscrupulously used to describe leather with "leather looking PU's"! So it's always best to have a good feel and to ask a question or two.

- "*Full leather.*" If your chair carries this label, it ought to be exactly what it says, not approximately accurate.

Finishing Flourishes: Delightful and Daft

This is where we can turn a lovely blank cow hide into leopard spots or zebra stripes. We can add one color or many colors, presenting our departed heifer with a completely new style that we hope the consumer will enjoy. We also hope it would have made the cow proud, although sometimes I am afraid that upholsterers call for effects that the cow would definitely frown at from its heavenly meadows.

Tribal tattoos have locked the look of the nineties into human hide—dodgy holiday tattoos can date quickly! But leather furniture is much more future-proof. Cowhide carries with it a lasting iconic look that holds fast the fashion and timeless finishes that will be appreciated by future generations. This iconic look can take a surprising amount of artifice to create!

Aniline dyes make for the most natural looking leather. They are beautiful, translucent, and warm. The problem is that your glass of red wine or your spaghetti bolognese will leave eternal stains. It is hard to clean. It produces the most marvelous patina over the years, if left unsullied by domestic accidents. Oh, and another thing—it will need weekly care for the next hundred years. Although it's so expensive that if you can afford to buy it you are probably already employing a housemaid who can take care of such things for you.

On that point, I once saw an incredibly beautiful full aniline sofa in Harrods of London (one of the most famously luxurious shops in the world). A creative customer had used his finger nail to draw a giant penis and balls onto the back cushion—pure toilet art at its finest! Someone had attempted to wipe it out which just added hair to the masterpiece. Aniline leather marks easily!

Semi-aniline dyes make leather more stain resistant (and finger-nail resistant!). It consists of a polymer surface coating that gives the hide more durability while still letting the leather look natural.

Perhaps, though, the most artifice goes into making new leather look old. *"Distressed leather"* finishes make it look like you've inherited the chair from a lineage started by the Tudors. The finish is sprayed on in patches and parts are randomly erased so that the dark dye reveals light leather patches "underneath." It is currently a hot trend amongst leather-chair-buyers, but it will be a trend that will blend comfortably into your home as the fake age blends into real age. Your grandchild will be glad to inherit it!

As a closing point on this topic, I would like to stress that you should think twice about the finish of the leather before buying into either upholstery or upholstery design. It is possible to print designs on leather, for instance. Think about that as carefully as you would think about getting a tattoo, though. Laser tattoo removal will not work on your leather sofa.

Fashion Trends in Cow-Sitting

When credit card meets card machine, people who buy leather are usually prospecting for something relatively timeless, but with a wide range of style options. In these times, a leather chair must carry a deep seat and well-upholstered arms, and look like it's been accommodating arses for at least a century. As an upholstery designer, there is a balancing game I have to play. I want to be creative—I *am* creative—but I need to *sell* what I create in order to *keep* creating. My clientele is inspired by novelty and freshness and fashion—but what ties every piece I design together, past and future, is luscious leather from the comfortable cow.

On the other hand, I have been able to introduce some significant changes in various areas and genres of design. The popularity of some of my work has allowed me to push the creative boundaries a little, as my designs meet a need to acquire furniture with classic lines that still express a fresh new vision. Changes in the mainstream market have to be infinitesimal, though, as public opinion crawls on to a new classic look.

Just before travel was inconvenienced by a global pandemic, I had the good fortune to be able to visit an old friend and do a research trip to the Milan leather fair in Italy. This market is predominantly for smaller fashion leather items, as the Lineapelle Milano' International Leather Fair at Rho focuses on the hungry market for designer bags and shoes. The contemporary upholstery market has switched almost entirely to being a contractor's market because of the sheer volume of leather needed to accommodate human bums. There's a lot less leather used in shoes and handbags, but a lot more profit!

The Fair, the largest in Italy, is nonetheless an incredible experience. I would highly recommend it to anyone with even the slightest interest in leather. It showcases an absolutely incredible range of creative leather design. At Lineapelle Milano you will encounter leather that has been altered, enhanced, and recreated to achieve fascinatingly creative results. I'm an experienced designer, and I was deeply impressed.

I went there as part of a project I was working on where I wanted to funk up my leather upholstery designs with splashes of intriguing leathers taken from the fashion industry. The Milan Leather Fair gave me a lot to think about. But that wasn't all. My friend then invited me to his partner's tannery in San Miniato, a small Tuscan town. There they create and process leathers beyond imagination for the leading fashion houses of today—Gucci, Versace, Dolce & Gabbana, and more.

Due to the reduced size of the panels of leather the fashion industry needs to create bags and shoes, they can afford a whole new level of exciting methodologies to create fabulous effects—for example embossing patterns into leathers with 1.2m plates using the center of hides. As the retail price of shoes and bags is so high, they can afford a level of wastage that the furniture industry could not cope with. Manipulating smaller sizes of leather also allows for a faster process, which in turn allows for an experimental/testing process to be completed much more quickly. I had a plethora of effects to choose from. They produce some sensational metallic effects—burnished copper to rusting iron. And they have the capacity to imprint visual imagery, incorporating Versace's signature style prints into sensational leather textures for bags and shoes alike.

As a furniture leather designer I had to do some careful cost-benefit analysis. If you make the product too expensive, it will look great in your showroom—but sales will be impeded. However, I found that even a small use of novelty leather in highlighting certain areas could achieve fascinating and inspiring results.

After salivating over the coolest reincarnated cows in the world, we naturally followed up by eating some of them. After we consumed some classic Italian cuisine, my friend took me to another leather supplier, a colleague of his who supplies leather for the swanky Hermes brand, a luxury French fashion house. The owner of the supply firm is a curious man with an intriguing studio. The entrance featured a large framed artistic photograph of a vagina. Inside, his glass walled office was brimming with pictures of himself jumping through muddy puddles with medals on!

The man might be eccentric, but his stock—!

He had the most supple leather a human hand could ever experience, a tantalizing buffet of tactile delight. I was completely confused by how the fifty or more pieces of tanned leather, all the same Hermes-signature brown color, could vary so much in texture and heft. They had figured out processes that produced leathers that delicately licked and fell through your fingers with an almost warm, buttery sensation. It was a sensory delight, like a whisky tasting experience, except with leathers. It was as if the leather left a lingering aftertaste—equivalent to vintage single malt whiskey "finish"—on the fingers, evolving in pleasure as the physical memory faded.

I complimented the owner on providing an experience I had rarely had. He of course agreed that his leather was the most unrivaled product on God's green earth. He indicated that I was to feel undeservedly welcome, as a mere mortal, to the paradisal permission bestowed upon me. But I guess he deserved to be a little arrogant. Given the prices he gets from Hermes, I presume that he is held in rather high esteem in the handbag trade.

My Italian expedition made me reflect a great deal about industry and fashion. The furniture industry will always have an element of fashion. Even though we're not quite at the cutting-edge of the fashion industry, we *are* getting closer, in our own way. Far from being a traditional staple, today's domestic furniture industry is all about the extension and expression we want to perceive in our living environments. Furniture is being seen as not merely functional, but expressive of our values and dreams. With ever-improving manufacturing methods, increasing competition, and broader choice, more and more people now feel that they can own a significant mark of their unique identity in their own environment. This is *my* damn cow!

It's All About the Animal

Understanding leather as an animal's skin is one of the most important things I wish I could impress on the world. First Nation Americans would always thank an animal they had killed in the hunt for its contribution to the life of the hunter. In the same spirit, I believe we should respect the cow, and commit ourselves to using its hide well.

I'm still amazed that purchasers and retailers of upholstery furniture hardly invest any time into learning more about the products and articles they are buying and selling. As I talk with people in the trade, I am disturbed by the inherent ignorance about the cow-ness of leather. I don't know whether it's lack of training or lack of interest, but I've had very senior buyers of upholstery leather furniture (for very large retailers) who seem to believe that cowhide originates in warehouses which lay eggs in the form of rolls of fabric, with no conception at all of leather's prior life!

Chapter 9:

It's a Hard Knock Life for the Herbivore

It is important to know how the cow you are sitting on was raised. How well we have learned to disassociate ourselves from the fact that it once walked and chewed (and chewed and chewed)!

Deliberate mistreatment of farm animals is a crime, although it does not carry much of a sentence. There are, sadly, many humans who should not be allowed to have responsibility for livestock. But they are fortunately the minority. All farmers at least *intend* to take good care of their cattle, because diseased and injured cows are not worth much. Also, however, cattle farmers in my experience actually *love* their big blundering bovines.

Let's get back to that preschool point-and-tell book for a moment. The reality is that the black-and-white cow on a green field is not the norm for cattle rearing. Internationally, we are much more likely to be dealing with dusty brown cows with big horns on a dusty brown piece of countryside. The percentage is skewed slightly in India, where so many people are disinclined to eat beef, but only about 10% of cows worldwide are bred for milk. And boy, do they produce milk! A Holstein cow, that archetypical black-and-white cow, can produce about 35L of milk per day. Other breeds produce *much* less, even cows that might be bred for milk rather than beef. In India, farmers are increasingly importing Holsteins because of their extraordinary yield.

With that in mind, let us segue off into what different animals are genetically grouped under the title "cow."

Highland Coos and Assorted Moos: An International Alphabet of Cows

There are two types of cow: *Bos Taurus Taurus* (bred for the cold) and *Bos Taurus Indicus* (bred for the heat). Cows have spread over the face of the earth and are almost as diverse as the human species, with 1,000 registered breeds. Here's an alphabet of cows just itching to be turned into a children's book!

- Aberdeen Angus/Ankole
- Brahman
- Charolais
- Dairy Shorthorn
- English Longhorn
- Friesian
- Guernsey
- Holstein, Highland, Hereford
- Iceland
- Jersey
- Kalmyk
- Limousin
- Masai
- Nguni
- Ongole
- Parda Alpina
- Qinchaun
- Riggit Galloway
- Simmental, Shorthorn

- Thai Fighting Bull
- Ukrainian Gray
- Vestland Fjord
- Wagyu, White Park
- Xingjiang Brown
- Yanhuang
- Zebu

Leather Terroir? Unique Properties of Unique Meadows

The quality of the leather in your upholsterer's hand depends a lot on where the cow came from. To start with, cows raised in colder climates will have less skin damage from insects. The thick hair of a Highland coo, that keeps it snug inside a warm cocoon in the Scottish snows, is also an added protection against horn pokes and barbed wire scratches. It's just a pity that their hides are so tiny! On the other hand, a country like South Africa, with its teeming herds of cattle, actually has to import hides for its shoe industry. The hot conditions mean that, despite all the ivermectin cattle dips and the incessant swishing of their tails, the poor beasts are constantly being bitten by hungry African insects.

As I have gone shopping for hides from around the world, I have come to realize that European continental cows deliver bigger hides—offering us a healthy 55 sq ft of usable, prime upholstery-ready skin. South American hides tend to be smaller. And of course Indian cows have that huge hump, which results in the processed hide having a large, characteristic hole at one end. A bit of a puzzler for the mail-clad leather cutters after a night on the town.

Cows are only bred for meat and milk, though. There is no breed that is bred for its leather alone. The hide is always a valuable by-product, which is why it was such a tragedy that during the COVID-19 pandemic, so many American hides had to be destroyed because the leather manufacturing industry shut down.

The bottom line is that although every animal has a hide, every hide gets judged on its merit by many assessors along the way. There are many factors to take into account. Cattle bred for beef tend to produce better skins than cattle bred for milk. Ox and heifer hides are more sought after than cowhides. Bull hide is thicker, and calf hide is thinner. And the higher grade the beef, the higher grade the skin will be. Generally, the more happy and healthy the cow has been, the better its hide will be. In Norway, for instance, you get fined if your cow turns up at the abattoir in bad condition. That legal deterrent, combined with the abandonment of barbed wire by Norse farmers, means that Norwegian hides command a good price.

Happy Herds of Contented Cows?

Cows, like humans, have been bred for a soft life. We have pathetic excuses for claws, and we have completely lost our bite-force. Likewise, cows have easily damaged hooves, intended for shuffling around in soft grasslands rather than galloping over stony steppes. This means that humans have to constantly make adjustments to accommodate their cows: we bred them soft, so we've got to coddle them.

Cow-Drink

Farmers know that a cow has to have about 50L of clean, fresh water a day. In some places this is easy to supply, and cows stand dreamily up to their hocks in crystal clear streamlets, drinking as much as they want. In dryer places, aqualogistics is more difficult. Some cattle, like the Brahman and Nguni, are more accustomed to limited water rations—but even they will die of dehydration in drought conditions.

Cow-Food

Food is the next concern for a cattle farmer and, of course, his cow. Cows are hungry animals. They need about 4% of their body weight in grass or hay per day. Um, let's see, four percent of, say, 600kg is—wait for it—24kg of grass per day! That's an entire airplane luggage allowance! They process this through four stomachs, chewing and rechewing as they contentedly process grass into leather, beef, and poo. Cows do not need nutrient-rich feeds. They need lots and lots of various grass products.

Some farmers devote entire fields to growing cow food. If the winters are too severe for the cattle to be outdoors, and if snow and ice cover the greenery, then silage becomes essential—that rich, anaerobically-fermented foodstuff that emerges slowly from the tarp-covered mountain of wet grass at one end of the barn. Alternatively, there is a thriving market for hay to feed cows. In dryer parts of the world, farmers have to buy feed during the dry season. Cows are browsers, which means that they have to be able to wrap their extraordinarily long tongues around the long grass-stalks to ingest it. No dainty nibbling like sheep and goats.

Cow-Vitamins

Cows need balanced diets. They mostly need sheer volume of fiber, but if their fodder is low in selenium or magnesium, farmers have to add it to their salt licks. Oh, and they need saltlicks! Balanced nutrition is an artform, and so nutritionists and agricultural chemists have come up with TMR, "Total mixed ration," that is fed to cows as they are milked or spread around the herd in some other creative way. Pregnant cows get a pregnancy diet. I suppose the stud bull gets a stud diet. Farmers who take this seriously have the happiest cows and most profitable product (Couse, 2018).

Mixed pasture is another way of ensuring a well-balanced diet, but that is only available for a small percentage of the world's cows. The pasture must, of course, not be so mixed that includes poisonous shrubs like oleander.

Medical Aid for Cows

Cows need a barn-full of medical care. Most of it is intended to stave off disease, like regular cow-dipping against insect infestations. However, cows are still prone to mysterious maladies like foot rot, blue tongue, and hardware disease (i.e. swallowing nails and bits of wire that damage that four-stomach food processor). Rural vets have a lot of traveling to do.

Another regular caregiver is the hoof trimmer. Farmers can mostly do this for themselves, but some really nasty things go wrong with cows' feet, especially when they are kept on concrete floors. The Popeye-forearmed hoof trimmers trim and grind hooves into balance, removing the odd embedded spark plug, and packing abscesses with antibiotics.

The frontline healer is the stock manager. This is a person who knows and loves the cow. In most parts of Africa, it's a little boy with a stick. They pick up immediately when the cow is off-color, and can instantly bring in expert assistance. They are in charge of the cow's general well being, giving injections when needed, moving the herd from place to place, making sure the animals get enough shade or shelter.

Very occasionally, an epidemic breaks out. Foot-and-mouth is one,—a horrible, incurable virus that requires traumatically instant culling and quarantine measures. There is a vaccine, thankfully, that stops cows from catching it. Agricultural policy is to ring-fence any outbreak by vaccinating every single cow in a wide swathe around the epicenter of the disease.

When there's a chance of a disease that can spread from cows to humans, things get considerably more jumpy. Those who lived in Britain between 1985 and 1987 are still not out of the shadow of bovine spongiform encephalopathy (Mad Cow Disease, which sounds like something Gary Larson thought up). You don't have to eat cow products to catch it, and it's highly dangerous. Fortunately, only about one person in a million catches it each year. In the greater scheme of things, we humans have benefited immensely more from the mild cowpox milkmaids used to contract. In 1796, Edward Jenner ingeniously figured out that people who had had *cowpox* did not get the killer disease *smallpox*. Untold millions of people have been saved from death because sleepy milkmaids leant their foreheads against the warm bums of their cows.

A Whole Range of Cattle Ranges

As we have looked at the varied faces of the cow, it has become clear that cows can thrive in various different habitats, so long as they have enough water, mixed grasses, and a salt lick. If they have a sympathetic human to nudge them around and talk to them kindly, and perhaps one or two musicians, then they will have lived a contented, fulfilling life. Cows are easy to please.

Do we please them? Yes and no.

Farmers generally *do* try to cherish their cows, because a contented cow is a cash cow. Most cattle are reared specifically for meat, and get sold for their meat and by-products as soon as they weigh enough. Heifers who are raised for their milk are only kept for five or six years, until their calving capacity and milk production declines. Then they too are sold off for meat and useful cow derivatives. The industry is not sentimental about allowing cows to live out their potential 15 years—cows are kept to serve certain human needs, and they then fulfill those needs. That does not amount to cruelty, though, because cows only live in the present. They do have memory for kind or cruel treatment, and for that farmers are answerable to a higher court if not to a legal one. But cows themselves have no anxiety about their future life and no premonitions of death. If the slaughter is done humanely, they live a contented life from birth to death.

In Northern climates, where cows have to be kept inside in winter, cows pick up many injuries from abrasive concrete floors and sharp steel fittings. There is a move to keep cows on rubber matting, and install flexible frames that cows don't catch their ankles on. It's fine if there's merely a suggestion of where a stall should be. Another way to make cows comfortable through an indoors winter is to keep them on deep sand. The test as to whether the cow is comfortable enough is to drop heavily on your own human knees onto the sand. If it's deep enough for the cow you will not hurt yourself!

Cows don't have to be physically hurt to be driven from place to place, because most of the time the herd moves like clockwork. They are preoccupied with their four stomachs, and unwilling to invest energy in thinking rebellious thoughts. Bulls and calves need a little more direct handling, though. Calves are energetic and curious. Bulls are, well, 700kg of "I'll do what I want when I want" attitude. But even if it is a climatic necessity, cows don't like being all penned up inside for the whole of winter. There are touching YouTube videos of cows being let out for the first time in spring, where you see their massive frames skipping and kicking their heels in the tender grass. Wherever possible, that is exactly where farmers keep them, happily foraging around during the day and dreamily chewing the cud under the stars at night.

When it comes to running large-scale beef herds, the process has to be more mechanized, although the received wisdom is still that cattle need human contact to be happy. However, things need to be organized, because pregnant cows or calves at various times of year demand differing feeding and treatment. Soil analysis and the foraging capacity of the land need to be well matched to stock numbers. A certain amount of mechanization is inevitable to manage the herd's environment to keep it comfortable.

Herding maneuvers related to milking, disease management and marketing need to be seamless and non-traumatic. One old cattle man says that you should never overcrowd pens leading to squeeze chutes. Cows get spooked when they realize they do not have the freedom to stampede, and then they hurt themselves against the steel bars. Forcing cows into dark buildings is also cruel—keep the lights bright, and put in as many skylights as you can afford. His next advice is not to encircle cattle when trying to herd them—that's like compressing atoms of Uranium-234. When they get too close together, they are liable to explode. Eons of breeding has not bred out the instinct to stampede away from circling predators. And don't use cattle prods! Cows are much happier if they get attracted into a stall with a food bucket than smacked with a jolt of electricity (Arrowquip, 2017).

Sadly, all these abuses are happening all the time. Never by the majority of cattle owners, but always by some. In better regulated countries these abuses are spotted and prosecuted. In less regulated countries, though, cattle sometimes live a hard and uncomfortable life. Humanity needs to raise its game. Cows are never cruel to humans.

Chapter 10:

Alternative Cows—a Leather Substitute?

It's no secret that I love leather. But I am not deaf to the clamor that the beef industry is not being responsible about its impact on the planet. I *do* think that we should urgently change our ways. I *don't* think that eliminating all the cows from the planet is the answer.

To start with, any recklessness on the part of the dairy, beef and leather industry is all one piece of our human recklessness across all industries. In order to get the most money, we want to spend as little as we can get away with on our environmental impact. Inaction by the mass does not, however, excuse inaction by the few. We are all obliged to do the best we can to make the world a better place.

So let's tackle some of the issues head-on.

Farting Cows and Greenhouse Gasses

Cow culture produces 10-15% of the gasses that are making us increasingly cozy in our global greenhouse. I accept that. Anybody who has spent time close to a cow knows that it is a remorselessly rumbling engine. Their ultra-high-fiber diet generates a *lot* of gas!

The Cow's Carbon Hoofprint

Beef on the plate (and by extension, leather on the sofa) costs a huge amount in greenhouse gasses released into the atmosphere. A lot of that comes from bovine flatulence, or to be accurate, bovine *burps*. It's a front-end emission! A lot of that carbon cost, however, comes from transport, industrial processing, and the felling of trees in the rainforests to clear ground for cow-supporting crops like grass.

Methane is the big baddie that can be blamed on the individual cow. There are millions of cows, producing ton upon ton of methane gas—about 350 liters of methane per day, per cow (Watts, 2019).

The Hunter's Off-Set?

It is interesting, though, to reflect that wild ungulates like bison, giraffe, and kudu emit comparable amounts of greenhouse gasses. I have not seen any research on this, but I do wonder whether we haven't just exchanged one ungulate for another. The vast herds of bison and wildebeest have been harried and hunted to a small fraction of their former pomp and glory. As human populations have exploded, though, we have replaced most of the missing herds with new herds of more biddable bovines. I wonder to myself—and this is nothing but a wonder at this stage—whether the total amount of methane is not much the same as it always was. In balance across reduced wild herds and increased domesticated herds, isn't the Earth's bovine flatulence level much the same as it ever was? In other words, the jolt of methane from cows is completely natural.

If that is so, that would mean that the burden of adjustment of greenhouse gasses should fall on the main culprit: fossil fuels, which produce 75% of the world's dangerous emissions anyway. Stop the factories farting fossil fuels, and leave the cows in their flatulent haze!

Poison Oozes Where Regulation Snoozes

I am not arguing that the leather industry is as pure as the driven snow. I suspect that factories might be somewhat inclined to only take the impact of their chimneys and drains if they know an incorruptible inspector might turn up and sniff their effluent. More money for less investment is the commercial creed, and it takes powerful, well-organized and well-intentioned regulators to ensure compliance with green laws.

In wealthier countries, where factory inspectors get paid good wages, this is mostly the case. We applaud the tidy tanneries and clean companies. But all is not as it seems. According to the theory of carbon off-setting, factories of any sort in clean countries can pay for their cleanliness by getting the majority of the dirty work done "elsewhere." Alternatively, factories in wealthy countries are allowed to carry on pumping out pollutants if they can pay a little money to some third world country to plant trees or something to "offset" their emissions by fixing the equivalent amount of carbon to that which the rich factory emmits. I hope that no tanneries or leather factories are doing this, but I fear that some might be.

Cost cutting is a constant threat to ethical leather production. Under pressure from retailers increasing their already very high margins, one tannery came up with a cheap new way of processing leather, using dimethyl fumarate (DMF). I don't know what happened in the testing and certification process, but lots of lovely cheap leather was snapped up by furniture retailers in the UK. Sadly, once the products started leaving the showrooms and being installed in homes, reports of allergic reactions began to roll in from hospitals around the British Isles. People were reporting rashes, burns and blisters (Stephensons, 2022)! The products were recalled, the leather was anathematized, DMF was summarily banned by law, and a popular UK leather furniture retailer dissolved. It was a brief lapse, but a dangerous one. It does demonstrate, however, how the big industry stakeholders pressure the upholstery business to take shortcuts with leather in the interests of greater profits. That's what regulatory boards are for!

One of the key issues in leather production is our tendency to prefer cheaper products from poorer countries, where the incentive to interfere in profit taking is lower, and regulatory efforts are much less secure. Is plausible deniability really the gold standard of environmental responsibility?

Ruminants vs. Rainforests?

Brazilians are cutting down the Amazon rainforests to grow grass for cattle. Brazilian ranchers jeer green-sensitive Europeans, of course, and ask them where the primordial forests of Europe have gone. If the Europeans have cut down all their own trees for European cattle, the argument goes, why interfere with the Brazilians for doing the same thing?

Cool. We can argue with each other until the grandchildren of the rich are starving on a gutted globe. There must be something we can do about making the world a little better, and my company certainly takes its sourcing policy seriously.

Which leads into what I call my "leather ethics."

Leather Ethics

I am not a lawyer or an ethics expert. I am, however, an ethical designer who specializes in leather. Since I literally have 'skin in the game,' I have had to think about these issues all through my career. It is true that I have a lot at stake, which inevitably colors my view. But that does not disqualify me from holding opinions and making choices. I won't say that I am a paragon of environmental virtue, but we all have to draw an ethical line in the sand whether we drive a car, fly in a plane, eat a hamburger—or upholster a sofa. What I offer here are my guiding principles.

I believe that we should seek a place where leather is sustainable within a global economy that is itself sustainable in every aspect.

Leather is Part of Our Human Heritage

The art and craft of leather working is one of our great human achievements. The creativity and comfort of leather furniture upholstery should not be lost.

Leather is a Circular Resource

Leather does not exploit a natural resource on a trajectory which leads to the complete exhaustion of that resource. Like grains, grapes, and trees, it is possible to produce leather in a circular, self-sustainable loop. Even though some unscrupulous leather bandits might not care, the industry does have *potential* to be globally sustainable.

Carbon Off-Setting

Carbon trading is a charade, a fraud perpetrated on the global community by rich manipulators. All industry should take responsibility for its own local sustainability, and the welfare of its own environment.

Less Beef and Less Leather

I should eat less beef and better beef, but not no beef.

Transparent Supply Chains

I insist on knowing where my leather comes from, and I will rather not buy from suppliers who are not being responsible for their own environments. Also, if I catch you being cruel to cows I will drop your leather like a hot cow-dung coal.

Costed-in Sustainability

I will work towards costing in the price of sustainability to my products. This will be a struggle because of needing to be competitive in order to stay in business, but I will do my best.

Change in Positioning

I will present my contribution to leather sustainability as part of my contribution to a sustainable world economy. I want you to show me what you are doing in that regard before you criticize where I have drawn my ethical lines.

Encouraging—Not Resisting—Research

The leather industry is obligated to encourage research into ways of reducing the carbon impact on the global environment. I will do all I can to promote such research, and to adopt leather produced using greener technologies.

Open to Innovation

I will actively experiment with alternative fabrics. I do not intend to replace leather, but to offer it as a choice amongst other sustainable upholstery materials.

Alternative Armchairs for the Anthropoid Arse

And that brings us to looking at alternative upholstery to leather.

I have had wide experience in using various fabrics other than leather in my career, although I always come back to sitting on cows. But I realize that the massive, growing leather industry will soon not be able to accommodate our insatiable desire for new things. There has to be an off-set, and it's up to creative designers like me to seek out those options. I'm constantly on the lookout for alternative materials to use *with* leather and *instead* of leather. Here's where I've got to so far.

Polymers

There are so many man-made materials that relieve the cow from being sat upon, and instead reassigned to, say, bedroom cosplay and Ann Summers whips!

Faux leathers made with PVC or the newer PU, are sometimes called "vegan leather," which I think is a remarkable piece of retail positioning. It certainly uses no animal products, but there is certainly more to be said about it! PU/PVC synthetic leather is already an integral part of the upholstery business. It's made by coating a fabric with a layer of PVC, which is then foamed, i.e. brought to the boil on a journey by conveyor belt through a long oven. These bubbles are fixed in place in the cooldown process, leaving the product with that spongy, leather-like feel. The process is completed by our old friend, the leather-texture embossing roller.

Synthetic leather does not have the live-skin feel of cowhide products, but it *looks* great, and is *much* cheaper. My problem is that although it potentially reduces the amount of cowhides we need, it is not in itself a circular product. It is part of the fossil fuels industry that is driving itself to exhaustion whilst encouraging our global climate to engulf island cultures and seaside resorts.

Natural Fibers and—Sand?

Some progress has been made in leather look-alike materials. Hugo Boss is using Pinatex experimentally, a leather alternative made from pineapples (Hahn et al., 2020). Another tough, embossable fabric is being produced from coffee grounds and sea shells. Mushrooms can also serve as a stretchy substance to turn into faux leather, while progress is being made into investigating linoleum and reconstituted abattoir discards. That last one can't be called vegan leather, I don't suppose.

I'm currently working with some incredible materials, however—one of which is 100% recyclable and made from *sand*. Unlike UP/PVC, it has all the properties of leather. It's too early to tell how well this is likely to go down with the buying public, but the products are stunning.

Also, if this wasn't a book about leather, I could go into silk and cotton and wool, which all produce sustainable fabrics that are beautiful and durable. As I promised in my introduction, they deserve their own book at some later date.

Bottom Line—the Bovine Balance

My mind is always bubbling with ideas. And solutions. If there are any ecological issues with the way we use leather, I am up for solving them—not by eradicating leather, but by developing healthy alternatives to use alongside it.

Sitting Comfortably

Let's sit together for a moment. I'd like to invite you into the warm embrace of my favorite, well-worn leather sofa with beer in hand, or perhaps a nice red wine decanting. Nestle your bum and back into an accommodating, form-fitting hollow and relax into the leather. You are now sitting on a cow. Comfy? I think so. We have been on an exploration of my memories in celebration of the cow.

In chapter one, I tried to show you how full of cow our world is, whether or not we are conscious of it.

In chapter two, I looked at the deep history we have with the cows we now sit on, immortalizing *them* on cave walls instead of pictures of our *chiefs*.

In chapter three, we licked our lips, mostly, over memories of meals made of beef bits all over the world.

In chapter five, I introduced you to the hyper-versatility of herbivore hide.

In chapter five, I tried to sketch out the enormous value the cow has for humans, *apart from* leather and beef!

In chapter six, I brought you with me to vomit in a tannery and learn how to produce leather from cowhide.

In chapter seven, I recalled my early experiences learning the trade, and demonstrated the importance of both a clear head and a chain mail glove.

In chapter eight, I showed how leather gets split and spliced.

In chapter nine, we had an overview of a cow's life.

And in chapter ten, I allowed you a glimpse into some of the ethical issues I face as an ungulate upholstery designer.

And so they lived happily ever after. I hope that I have brought you to the same comfortable position I am in, sitting on cows. I hope I have inspired you in some small way by sharing my deep affection and respect for the cow. I would be delighted if you shared my pleasure in the wonderful dining versatility beef offers. I would be especially pleased if you engaged physically and personally with the multitude of tactile and olfactory sensations leather has to offer.

So unwind and relax. Succumb to the smooth comfort of the sofa, and reflect on the wonders of the cow, secure in the embrace of leather. As the golden fingers of the evening sunlight reach in under the eaves and slant through the windows, that is where I would like to leave you.

Sitting on a cow.

THE END

References

AIAC. (2020). *AIAC paper (20-11-01) - overview of 2019-20 cattle related incidents investigated*. HSE. https://www.hse.gov.uk/aboutus/meetings/iacs/aiac/241120/overview-2019-20-cattle-related-incidents-investigated.pdf

Arrowquip. (2017, June 6). *Common Cattle Handling Mistakes*. Arrowquip. https://arrowquip.com/blog/livestock-handling/common-cattle-handling-mistakes

Baynes, C. (2018, December 4). *500-year-old skeleton wearing leather boots found in River Thames*. The Independent. https://www.independent.co.uk/news/science/archaeology/skeleton-river-thames-leather-boots-london-bermondsey-archaeology-a8667001.html

BizVibe. (2020, April 29). *Top 10 Largest Leather Producing Countries 2020 | Top Leather Exporters & Importers*. Bizvibe Blog. https://blog.bizvibe.com/blog/top-10-largest-leather-producing-countries

Chen, W., Chen, Z., & Shan, Z. (2021, July 20). *Development of aldehyde and similar-to-aldehyde tanning agents - Wenlong Chen, Zhijun Chen, Zhongzhen Long, Zhihua Shan, 2021*. SAGE Journals. https://journals.sagepub.com/doi/abs/10.1177/00405175211023813?ai=1gvoi&mi=3ricys&af=R&

ColourLock. (2022). *Tannins - Tanning agents*. Leather Dictionary. https://www.leather-dictionary.com/index.php/Tannins

Cook, R. (2022). *World Beef Consumption: Ranking Of Countries (USDA)*. Beef2Live. https://beef2live.com/story-world-beef-consumption-ranking-countries-164-106879

Couse, A. (2018). *How often does a cow see a doctor? Just to give you some perspective, people visit the doctor's office an average of 4 times a.* Amazon S3. https://s3.amazonaws.com/assets.cce.cornell.edu/attachments/18015/cow_sees_doctor_100816.pdf?1475858611

Cummins, E. (2019, October 28). *America's obsession with meat, explained.* Popular Science. https://www.popsci.com/why-americans-eat-so-much-meat/

Department for Environment, Food & Rural Affairs. (2021, March 25). *Farming statistics: Livestock populations at 1 December 2020 - UK.* GOV.UK. https://assets.publishing.service.gov.uk/government/uploads/system/uploads/attachment_data/file/973322/structure-dec20-ukseries-25mar21i.pdf

Farr, S. (2021). *10 Common Products That Contain Hidden Cow Parts.* One Green Planet. https://www.onegreenplanet.org/animalsandnature/common-products-that-contain-hidden-cow-parts/

Friedrik, C. (2021, November 17). *What Is a Tannery? | The Leather Tanning Process.* Carl Friedrik. https://www.carlfriedrik.com/blogs/magazine/what-is-a-tannery

Geggel, L. (2022, January 11). *Rare 'bionic' armor discovered in 2500-year-old China burial.* Live Science. https://www.livescience.com/rare-leather-armor-found-china-burial

Gurunavi. (2017). *Japanese Beef: 13 Best Dishes to Try When Visiting Japan.* https://gurunavi.com/en/japanfoodie/2017/11/japanese-beef-13-best-dishes-to-try-when-visiting-japan.html?__ngt__=TT12d68f075000ac1e4ae72c9mTeo5aZBgwktC86JQHETC

Hahn, J., Kwaning, D., & Abloh, V. (2020, October 16). *Six animal leather alternatives made from plants and food waste.* Dezeen. https://www.dezeen.com/2020/10/16/leather-alternatives-vegan-materials-design/

Handwerk, B. (2018, November 7). *World's Oldest Known Figurative Paintings Discovered in Borneo Cave.* Smithsonian Magazine. https://www.smithsonianmag.com/science-nature/worlds-oldest-known-figurative-paintings-discovered-borneo-cave-180970747/

Jarus, O. (2013, February 26). *Ancient shoes found hidden in Egyptian temple.* NBC News. Retrieved March 31, 2022, from https://www.nbcnews.com/news/all/ancient-shoes-found-hidden-egyptian-temple-flna1c8572009

Levine, J., Als, C., & Svensson, K. (2017). *Europe's Famed Bog Bodies Are Starting to Reveal Their Secrets.* Smithsonian Magazine. https://www.smithsonianmag.com/science-nature/europe-bog-bodies-reveal-secrets-180962770/

Liberty Leather. (2021). *The Incredible History of Leather.* Liberty Leather Goods. https://www.libertyleathergoods.com/history-of-leather/

Mayo Clinic. (2018). *Anxiety disorders - Symptoms and causes.* Mayo Clinic. https://www.mayoclinic.org/diseases-conditions/anxiety/symptoms-causes/syc-20350961

The Met. (2022). The Metropolitan Museum of Art. https://www.metmuseum.org/art/collection/search/591433

Nera Tanning. (2020). *Leather Tanning.* Nera Tanning. https://www.neratanning.com/leather-tanning/?gclid=CjwKCAjwrqqSBhBbEiwAlQeqGsLWm9FqMwioZwWJ7ulFTA0-9EEgGA2riYtjXceY2BaRzAxcX9bz8RoCV24QAvD_BwE

Olesen, J. (2020). *Fear of Cows or Cattle Phobia - Bovinophobia or Taurophobia*. FearOf.Net. https://www.fearof.net/fear-of-cows-or-cattle-phobia-bovinophobia-or-taurophobia/

Oraon, L. (2013). *Pasteurization*. Dairy Knowledge Portal. https://www.dairyknowledge.in/article/pasteurization

Pinkowski, J. (2021). National Geographic. https://www.nationalgeographic.com/history/article/tzi-the-iceman-what-we-know-30-years-after-his-discovery?loggedin=true

Rocha, V. (2015, April 20). *120-pound Sacramento woman sets record by eating 3 72-ounce steaks*. Los Angeles Times. https://www.latimes.com/local/lanow/la-me-ln-72oz-steak-eating-record-20150420-story.html

Science Daily. (2012, March 27). *DNA traces cattle back to a small herd domesticated around 10500 years ago*. ScienceDaily. https://www.sciencedaily.com/releases/2012/03/120327124243.htm

Stephensons. (2022). *Chemical at Centre of Defective Sofas to be Banned Stephensons Solicitors LLP*. Stephensons Solicitors LLP. https://www.stephensons.co.uk/site/news_and_events/firmsnews/chemical_at_centre_of_defective_sofas_to_be_banned

Swanson, A. F. (2015, August 20). *Food Waste And Beef Fat Will Be Making Airplanes Soar*. NPR. Retrieved April 1, 2022, from https://www.npr.org/sections/thesalt/2015/08/20/433193445/food-waste-and-beef-fat-will-be-making-airplanes-soar

Watts, G. (2019, August 7). *The cows that could help fight climate change*. BBC. https://www.bbc.com/future/article/20190806-how-vaccines-could-fix-our-problem-with-cow-emissions

Printed in Great Britain
by Amazon

Sitting on Cows!

our love for leather

Matt Arquette